REBEL

REBEL

FOLLOWING JESUS WHEN THE WORLD WALKS THE OTHER WAY

ANNE WILSON

W Publishing Group

An Imprint of Thomas Nelson

Rebel

Copyright © 2026 Anne Wilson

All rights reserved. No portion of this book may be reproduced, stored in a retrieval system, or transmitted in any form or by any means—electronic, mechanical, photocopy, recording, scanning, or other—except for brief quotations in critical reviews or articles, without the prior written permission of the publisher.

Published by W Publishing, an imprint of Thomas Nelson, 501 Nelson Place, Nashville, TN 37214, USA.

Published in association with the literary agency of WTA Media, LLC., Franklin, Tennessee.

Thomas Nelson titles may be purchased in bulk for educational, business, fundraising, or sales promotional use. For information, please email SpecialMarkets@ThomasNelson.com.

Unless otherwise noted, Scripture quotations are taken from The Holy Bible, New International Version®, NIV®. Copyright © 1973, 1978, 1984, 2011 by Biblica, Inc.® Used by permission of Zondervan. All rights reserved worldwide. www.zondervan.com. The "NIV" and "New International Version" are trademarks registered in the United States Patent and Trademark Office by Biblica, Inc.®

Scripture quotations marked CSB are taken from the Christian Standard Bible®, Copyright © 2017 by Holman Bible Publishers. Used by permission. Christian Standard Bible® and CSB®, are federally registered trademarks of Holman Bible Publishers.

Scripture quotations marked ESV are taken from the ESV® Bible (The Holy Bible, English Standard Version®). Copyright © 2001 by Crossway, a publishing ministry of Good News Publishers. Used by permission. All rights reserved.

Scripture quotations marked NASB are taken from the New American Standard Bible® (NASB). Copyright © 1960, 1962, 1963, 1968, 1971, 1972, 1973, 1975, 1977, 1995, 2020 by The Lockman Foundation. Used by permission. www.lockman.org.

Scripture quotations marked NASB1995 are taken from the New American Standard Bible®. Copyright © 1960, 1971, 1977, 1995 by The Lockman Foundation. Used by permission. All rights reserved. www.lockman.org.

Italics in Scripture indicate the author's emphasis.

Any internet addresses, phone numbers, or company or product information printed in this book are offered as a resource and are not intended in any way to be or to imply an endorsement by Thomas Nelson, nor does Thomas Nelson vouch for the existence, content, or services of these sites, phone numbers, companies, or products beyond the life of this book.

ISBN 978-1-4003-5541-9 (audiobook)
ISBN 978-1-4003-5540-2 (ePub)
ISBN 978-1-4003-5539-6 (TP)

Without limiting the exclusive rights of any author, contributor, or the publisher of this publication, any unauthorized use of this publication to train generative artificial intelligence (AI) technologies is expressly prohibited. HarperCollins also exercise their rights under Article 4(3) of the Digital Single Market Directive 2019/790 and expressly reserve this publication from the text and data mining exception.

HarperCollins Publishers, Macken House, 39/40 Mayor Street Upper, Dublin 1, D01 C9W8, Ireland (https://www.harpercollins.com)

Library of Congress Cataloging-in-Publication Data on File

Art direction: Meg Schmidt | Cover Design: Meg Schmidt | Interior Design: Kristina Juodenas

Printed in the United States of America

26 27 28 29 30 LBC 5 4 3 2 1

CONTENTS

INTRODUCTION

For several years now, the Lord has been leading me into deeper levels of surrender and trust, both of which are lived out through obedience to His Word. At times, obeying the Lord is easy and automatic. But not always. There are moments when obeying the Lord feels like I'm walking a lonely path, against the flow of the world around me. Sometimes I must choose to obey in the face of fears, negativity, and seemingly impossible situations. As God calls me deeper into the reality of His kingdom on earth, I long to follow Him, no matter the cost. It is not always easy and I do not do it perfectly, but I can honestly say that following Him is always worth it.

Many of my steps in obedience to Jesus have involved speaking up and speaking out for the Lord and not hiding or watering down the truth. As you probably already know, this can be very scary. Through this process, God has brought me to new levels of both surrender to His will and courage to take a stand. It was out of this journey with the Lord that I wrote my second album, *REBEL*. What the Lord does in my own heart and life flows out through my music, and He has been showing me that following Him will often mean looking like a rebel to the world around me. There is a cost to following Jesus. It involves surrendering our own comfort, pride, reputation, and desires. But what He gives in return far exceeds anything we could lay down for Him.

Recently, I could sense that it was time to be bold and write about what has been burning in my heart for some time now. The world around us grows more confusing and deceptive by the day. Truth is being obscured and twisted. You can't even watch a funny video online without questioning if it is real or if it was made with AI. Meanwhile, the political climate is increasingly hostile and polarized, and Christianity is under attack across the globe. Many call what is good *evil* and what is evil *good*. What better time than now for us to talk about what it really means to follow Jesus and bring His light to a dark world. People across the globe and even right next door to you desperately need Jesus . . . and desperately need someone who is unafraid to speak truth.

If these thoughts stir something in your soul, or even if you're just curious what I mean by being a rebel for Christ, this book is for you. Whether you are already pursuing the deeper things of God, or you haven't yet decided to follow Jesus, or you're somewhere in between, we all need encouragement to follow His Way. It matters to know we're not alone in this. I pray that as you journey with me through these pages, the Lord Himself will speak to you and inspire you. I'm honored to get to share a little of my journey with you, but it really means nothing without the Holy Spirit working through (or maybe in spite of) my words to make His call real in your own life.

I'm excited to link arms with you, friends, and follow our Savior together, come what may.

–Anne

CHAPTER 1

WHAT IS A REBEL?

"Anne Claire Wilson, what is on your face?" my mom asked. "Did you eat a fudge popsicle without getting my permission?" Her eyes narrowed as she looked me up and down.

I stood facing her in our kitchen without fear, as only a three-year-old can do. Dressed up in my full ballerina outfit, I shook my messy blond piggy tails and from a fudge-lined mouth declared loudly, "You are not the boss of *me*!"

"Oh no, young lady, actually I *am* the boss of you," Mom said. "God made your daddy and me the bosses of you. *We* are in charge."

After hearing her stern correction, I raised my

eyebrows and did what came naturally to me at that moment. Obviously, it was the perfect time to strike a ballerina pose.

This was not the first time my mom had heard me say those words, nor would it be the last. According to my parents, it was quite common for me to rip my pacifier out of my mouth, glare at them, and say my favorite phrase: "You are not the boss of me!" I may have been the baby of our family, but I did not like being told what to do by anyone. If I'm honest, I still don't.

Although I like to meet and even try to exceed expectations, I also have a bit of a rebellious streak. I don't automatically go with the crowd. In fact, I often enjoy doing just the opposite of what everyone else is doing. If I feel that a situation or conversation is not right, I won't join in, even if it means facing rejection. I almost relish it. And when it comes to being told what to do, I prefer to follow my own inclination, as evidenced by my toddler declarations.

This rebellious tendency easily could have led me down a dangerous path in life, but God had other plans. I am so thankful for His grace in drawing me to Himself early in life, before that desire to rebel against authority took too great a hold. My parents faithfully directed me toward following God from the day I entered this world, but I chose Jesus for myself when I was in seventh grade. When I gave my life over in surrender to Jesus, that included my bent toward going my own way. Under the power of the Holy Spirit, what could have been my downfall became a strength instead. God uses my desire to go against the flow to give me strength to stand for Him. I know this power is not of my own making. It is God's creation of my personality in submission to His perfect ways and fueled by His strength. I am learning to be a rebel *for* Christ.

WHAT IS A REBEL?

In the Christian world, the word *rebel* can have somewhat scandalous connotations, referring to someone who goes against all rules, structure, and decorum. Rebels are seen as mavericks who insist on doing things their own way. Parents shudder at the thought of their child going through a rebellious stage, and we pray for those who are in rebellion against God. So why would I make this word the title of my album and title song, as well as the central theme of my current ministry? The answer is both simple and yet full of meaning.

A young man recently asked me in an interview what

I meant by being a "rebel." After I gave him my quick summary, he nodded and simply said, "Oh, so you mean just being a Christian?"

Yes! That is exactly what I mean. And yet somehow, many of us in this modern American world of Christianity have lost some of the profound essence of being a follower of Christ. We've watered Christianity down to just being nice and going to church. But I think being a true follower of Jesus isn't always "nice" or tidy, and it definitely involves going outside the safe walls of the church. Being a Christian often means we look like rebels in the eyes of the world. But then, that's how Jesus lived.

JESUS WAS A REBEL?

The way Jesus entered our human world shattered people's preconceptions about who the Messiah would be and what He would do. God had long promised a savior to the Jewish people, whom they would call the Messiah. The religious leaders of the time knew all the prophecies about Him, but they added on their own expectations that He would be a powerful military leader and a mighty king on the earth. Jesus is both of those things, but He fulfills those roles in a greater and more eternal way than most people could understand at that time. They expected an immediate revolution for their nation. Instead, Jesus came as a baby, born in a barn, and through His life and death brought revolution for the whole of humanity.

I can't pretend to know all the intentions of God's heart in choosing the place and manner of Jesus' birth, but that unexpected arrival profoundly demonstrated both His humility and His humanity. The greatest Man to ever walk the earth, the King of all kings, and the Creator of heaven and earth came as a fragile baby, born to an unwed teenage girl. God was not worried about meeting the expectations of people but rather with fulfilling His Word and offering salvation to His people. Even Jesus' birth appears to be a clear rebellion, if you will, against the ways men would try to control Him and fit Him into their own religious boxes and preconceived ideas. The men of His day had a narrow view of a temporary kingdom. Jesus established an eternal kingdom that changed history and humankind forever.

When He was just twelve years old, Jesus stayed behind in Jerusalem while His earthly parents headed back home. But here's an important little detail: Jesus didn't tell His parents He was staying behind. Their family had been in Jerusalem for the Feast of the Passover, and when the days of celebration were over, they packed up and started their journey home. I can envision hundreds of thousands of people leaving the city. Imagine New York City at rush hour! A full day into the trip home, Joseph and Mary (Jesus' earthly parents) realized He was missing. How in the world had they not realized that for an entire day? The Bible says that they assumed He was somewhere in the caravan of people, maybe hanging out with His cousins. I know that's where I'd be. But after not seeing Him for many hours, they began to grow suspicious and started looking around for Him. He was nowhere to be found, and no one had seen Him since leaving Jerusalem. His parents rushed back to Jerusalem as fast as those donkeys could go.

Three days later, Jesus' parents found Him in the temple, talking with the Jewish teachers called rabbis. Pause for a second and let this story become real to you. Imagine His terrified parents running around the city, frantic to find their preteen son, asking everyone they could where Jesus was. For three whole days. With every passing hour, their fear mounted. Their stomachs churned, hearts pounded, and minds raced with a panic no parent ever wants to experience. But get this:

They hadn't just lost their own beloved son; they had lost the Son of God.

When Joseph and Mary finally found Jesus, they must have been overwhelmed with relief to the point of tears . . . and anger at what He had put them through. Here's how I see it in my mind's eye: They sprinted to Jesus and swept Him up in their arms as all the pent-up fear came rushing out. They peppered Him with questions about why He had stayed behind and why in the world He hadn't told them. Jesus' response might surprise you. "'Why were you searching for me?' he asked. 'Didn't you know I had to be in my Father's house?'" (Luke 2:49).

Does that sound *rebellious* to you? What if, as a kid, you had disappeared for days at a time and gave that response to your parents? I shudder at the thought. It helps the story come alive when we imagine how it must have felt to really experience it. But don't forget—we are not Jesus. To grasp what He was doing, we have to look at this with the full understanding of who Jesus is. We know based on Scripture that Jesus never sinned: "Therefore, since we have a great high priest who has ascended into heaven, Jesus the Son of God, let us hold firmly to the faith we profess. For we do not have a high priest who is unable to empathize with our weaknesses, but we have one who has been tempted in every way, just as we are—yet he did not sin" (Hebrews 4:14–15).

Jesus was perfect and holy, even as a man living in this fallen world and even as a twelve-year-old kid. So what was this seeming rebellion all about? Jesus was obeying a higher authority, His heavenly Father. He wasn't rebelling against His parents but rather was following the call of God. In the face of Joseph and Mary's very real and understandable human emotions, Jesus spoke a higher truth and reminded them of who He was (and is). He is the Son of God, who came to earth with a very clear mission. Nothing and no one could stop Him.

When His ministry on earth began, Jesus was just thirty years old, and it ended when He was thirty-three. In three short years, He changed the world. And not only the world at that time—He changed history and the future. Even our calendar revolves around His life on earth. The years before Jesus count down to His birth (BC stands for "before Christ"), and the years after His birth count up to His coming return (AD stands for *anno Domini*, which is Latin for "in the year of our Lord").[1] Jesus is the central figure in all of time and history. He revolutionized humanity's relationship with God.

In those few years of ministry, Jesus shattered many expectations and appeared to be such a rebel and outlaw that they eventually killed Him in the manner of a criminal. In his profound book on the person of Jesus, *Beautiful Outlaw*, John Eldredge put it this way: "You understand that by this point, the authorities think he [Jesus] is far too dangerous. And he is. In their minds, he is continually breaking the law and encouraging others to do so. They see him as an outlaw; they certainly end up hanging him like one."[2] Let's look at a few reasons they viewed Jesus as a rebel.

Jesus healed on the Sabbath, which the Jewish leaders thought was breaking the law of the Sabbath. He drew large crowds when He spoke, which infuriated the religious leaders and filled them with jealousy. He shared incredible truths about worship with a Samaritan woman and then sent her off to be the first missionary to her city. Keep in mind: Samaritans were hated by Jews, and Jewish men of the time were not supposed to speak to women, especially not Samaritan women of questionable morals. But Jesus burst through these man-made rules to achieve His higher purpose.

Thousands gathered to see Jesus, even in the face of Roman occupation. This alone was a very dangerous act because it could have been interpreted as insurrection! He ate with sinners and outcasts. He chose uneducated fishermen to be His disciples. He healed every kind of illness and delivered people from demons. He honored women and welcomed them among His chosen followers. He walked on water, turned water into wine, multiplied bread for thousands, and drove greedy people out of the temple with whips. He told the religious leaders they were whitewashed tombs and sons of the devil! He touched lepers—sick people who were not allowed near "clean" people, let alone to be touched by them.

Scandalous. Rebellious. In all the right ways.

But Jesus wasn't a rebel for the sake of rebellion. In fact, quite the opposite. He was on a mission from God, determined to do the Father's will. He came to destroy lies and sin and death. He lived a life of radical obedience to and dependence upon Father God. And as He did that, the political *and* religious leaders of the day saw Him as a threat to their power, control, and glory. He was dangerous . . . to the darkness. He was a rebel and an outlaw . . . to the unfounded traditions and rules of man. These people lied about Him and tried to kill Him more than once. They mocked Him and tried to humiliate Him. But He kept His eyes on the Father and on their great plan of redemption for the world. Jesus had a reward in mind that made it all worth it. What was that reward? It was you. And it was me. Take a look at what the author of Hebrews said about His suffering:

> Let us run with endurance the race that is set before us, fixing our eyes on Jesus, the author and perfector of faith, who *for the joy set before Him* endured the cross, despising the shame, and has sat down at the right hand of the throne of God. For consider Him who has endured such hostility by sinners against Himself, so that you will not grow weary and lose heart. (12:1–3 NASB1995)

Jesus came for us, fiercely intent on rescuing us from the kingdom of darkness and bringing us into His kingdom and His family. This is worth repeating: Nothing and no one could stop Him.

If we follow Jesus and fix our eyes on Him, we should expect the world to treat us in a way similar to how it treated Him. Our goal should be not to take that rejection personally but to align ourselves with Jesus and His mission on earth. The Bible says, "Dear friends, do not be surprised at the fiery ordeal that has come on you to test you . . . but rejoice inasmuch as you participate in the sufferings of Christ, so that you may be overjoyed when his glory is revealed" (1 Peter 4:12–13). Jesus Himself promised that we will face hardships when He said, "In this world you will have trouble. But take heart! I have overcome the world" (John 16:33).

I've been familiar with these Bible verses for a long

time, so I knew what was coming when I began to step out in Jesus' name and share His message of hope with the world outside the walls of the church.

A NEW STAGE

Alabama in the summertime is a unique combination of lush beauty and oppressive, humid heat. It was one of these scorching days in the summer of 2022 in Cullman, Alabama, when I stood backstage in a panic at what I was about to do. Fifty thousand people waited on the other side of the stage for me to bring my opening act to Rock the South, a country music festival that draws an energetic crowd of country music–loving folks. Some of the fans would appreciate my music and my message, I was pretty sure of that. But many of them wouldn't even understand, let alone appreciate, what I was about to bring to that stage. They were there to party, and I was there to preach.

What was I doing, standing there in my cute—but modest—outfit, with my message of Jesus' salvation? All the other women were scantily clad in outfits that flaunted their feminine attributes. The other acts were amazingly talented, but they weren't carrying the same message I was or living the same lifestyle. The whole atmosphere was one of partying and reckless abandon. I didn't fit in at all, and I was shaking in my ruffles and sparkly boots.

I knew that when I walked out on that stage, I'd face confusion from the crowd, if not mockery. Perhaps even some hatred. I was just a twenty-year-old girl from the Bluegrass who loved to sing about Jesus. Doubts overwhelmed my mind. How could I face fifty thousand wild fans? Did I have the courage to bring the light of Jesus into this dark world? Who was I that they would listen to me? What if they booed me right off that stage or threw things at me? I seriously thought they might.

My parents were there with me, behind that stage, as they always are. They could see that I was too frightened to walk out. Although I had performed at big Christian festivals before, never had I done a country festival like this. It felt like I was having a mild panic attack—heart racing, body shaking, and breath coming in shallow gasps. I was terrified.

But truth prevailed. First, my parents spoke the truth to me that God had brought me to this moment and He would give me what I needed when I needed it. They were right. I *knew* that God had called me to play this festival. I refused to disobey my heavenly Father.

Doing His will matters more to me than being accepted, even by thousands of people. So I did it. I did it scared, but I still did it.

Second, truth prevailed out on that stage. I did my very best to boldly share the gospel of Jesus Christ and to stay true to the call of God on my life. No matter what. I couldn't control the results from the crowd, but I spoke the truth of God that day.

I had initially been excited to have the opportunity to play Rock the South. I love country music to the core of my being! But it quickly became one of the hardest and least enjoyable venues I've ever played. Hold on, friends. There is another "but" coming . . .

But God had a plan.

While I was onstage, dripping sweat in the sweltering heat, feeling like I might pass out, and facing a wild crowd, God spoke to my heart. In that moment, I knew that He was calling me to bring the light of Jesus into the arena of country music, not as a one-time show but as a ministry.

Up to that point, I was a Christian artist with a country style. People did not fully consider me a country artist, but I knew in my soul that that was about to change. God did not tell me how or when the change was coming, just that He was directing me down a new path. I know His voice. It is sweeter to me than any other voice in the world, and I heard it that day. This was a pivotal moment for me. My heart, which had just been filled with fear, was now filled with joy at the thought of being a light for Jesus in country music. Even the thought of suffering for Him made me excited. That is part of the full Christian life! We are called to take up our cross and follow Jesus.

FOLLOWING HIS CALL

James, the brother of Jesus, wrote in his letter to the Jewish church that we should, "Consider it pure joy, my brothers and sisters, whenever you face trials of many kinds, because you know that the testing of your faith produces perseverance" (1:2–3). There is value, even joy, in suffering for Christ. If our Master was ridiculed, we will be too. If He was misunderstood, we should expect the same. If they called Him a rebel and an outlaw, get ready to be labeled with similar words if you follow Jesus.

This Christian life is not an easy one. But it is an incredible one. It's an epic journey of faith and adventure. There will be hardships, and there will be peace.

Jesus promised both. But just like Jesus endured inconceivable pain for the joy set before Him, we, too, can know that we have a great reward. I challenge you to read the New Testament and look for the word *reward*. Depending on which version you're reading, it shows up around twenty-six times. You'll be amazed at how much God encourages us with promises of eternal rewards if we obey and follow Him. Here is one example I love: "Blessed are you when people insult you, persecute you and falsely say all kinds of evil against you because of me [Jesus]. Rejoice and be glad, because great is your reward in heaven" (Matthew 5:11–12).

After that moment onstage in Alabama, I was genuinely excited to see how God was going to make a space for me in this new arena. I felt more ready than ever to see this scripture prove true in my life.

AN OPEN DOOR

My entrance into the country music world came sooner than I anticipated. By the end of that same year, my manager, Matthew West, came to me with the opportunity to sign with a country music label, Universal Music Group Nashville, for the creation of my next album. I was already in a long-term contract with Capital Christian, so this would be a unique partnership for a single album. I was thrilled with the news! I already knew that I wanted my sophomore album to have a strong country sound, so this was perfect. And it was right in line with what God had already told me.

There was, however, one concern in my mind that loomed large enough that I needed to voice it to Matthew. Even though this was a huge opportunity for me, I had one major condition. "Matthew," I said, "I know I'm meant to be a country artist, but I will not do this deal if they make me change. I have to stay true to who I am and to what God has called me to do." I had decided in advance that I would not budge on this and planted my flag in the ground. If they tried to change me or my message about Jesus, there was no deal.

Not much time passed before I met people from Universal Nashville, including the CEO. "Anne, we love what you do," she said. "We want you to stay just the way you are. Be authentic."

I was ecstatic to hear her say that. Peace began to permeate my soul. Her next words, though, blew me away. She looked me in the eye and said, "Anne, we need you to bring God back to country music."

Bring God back to country music. Friends, let's pause

here for a moment. We all have places in our worlds and in our hearts that we need to open up to God and invite Him into. Do not pass by this statement casually. I encourage you to take a few minutes and ask the Lord to help you see the areas in your world where you need to bring Jesus. Is there something in your life that you're keeping separate? Is there a wounded place in your heart that is locked down? I encourage you to bring Jesus into those very places and see what happens next.

When I heard the CEO tell me I needed to bring God back to country music, I felt like it was almost too good to be true! I knew that was exactly what God wanted for me next, but to hear this executive in the industry actually say the words was beyond my expectations! It could not be clearer that God was opening a door for me into country music. The peace that had started to fill me settled like a warm blanket for the rest of that meeting. I knew this was it. I was about to walk through this door and into a new world of music and ministry. I have always loved country music, but I had never been in the industry. And now I was getting the chance to walk in, not only as a female artist but also carrying the name of Jesus with me everywhere I placed my foot. It was time to step outside the walls of the church and tell the world about my Jesus.

NO COMPROMISE

After that meeting, events began to happen quickly for me in the world of country music. We got a contract in place, announced it to the world, and started work on my new album. In the weeks and months that followed that announcement, many people involved in the country music world approached me with excitement. One after another, they told me that they really needed me to bring God back to country music. I won't lie—it felt great to hear this. But I also held those words lightly. I wondered if these people really meant what they were saying or if they were just kind words offered because people knew it's what I would want to hear.

In the midst of all that busyness and wondering, God reminded me of an important moment that had taken place during my tour with Casting Crowns in the fall of 2022. Every day of this tour, we all joined together for a time of prayer and encouragement. During one of those daily prayer times, Mark Hall, the lead singer for Casting Crowns, began to speak on the missions different artists have. Some artists are called to minister to the body of Christ, he told us. This is a vital ministry to believers. And some artists are called to minister to non-Christians. This, too, is essential in the kingdom of

God. His words hit my heart with the power of God's Spirit. I knew they were for me.

I have felt a pull to take the name of Jesus into the world ever since I was saved in the seventh grade. Even back when I was that young, I would go with Pastor Cameron and other classmates to the local mall to pray for strangers. We shared Jesus' love and offered to pray for anything they needed. Cameron always encouraged us that we could bring the kingdom of God to the world, no matter what our age!

"You can do anything for Christ!" Cameron would say. "You are never too young to share about Jesus! You are never too young for God to work through you!" He had an infectious way of encouraging us and bolstering our faith. I believed him. I wanted to tell the world about Jesus. And we did. Sometimes when we prayed for people, we saw instantaneous healings! That forever marked me and took my faith to a deeper level. When you see God do a miracle right in front of your very eyes, you never forget it. There is nothing like the thrill of watching Jesus pour out His love on someone's life.

And here I was, eight years later, being given the chance to take the name of Jesus to a section of the world near and dear to my heart. God used those memories and the words of Mark and Cameron to confirm for me once again His direction for my life. I realized that all the people who were telling me they needed me to bring God back to country music weren't just saying what they thought I wanted to hear. They were speaking truth. They meant it. God meant it.

I didn't know how it would all play out, but I knew I was following God. And that is enough for me. I was also pretty sure that there would be many struggles along the way. I expected that some people would not accept me or my message in the country music world. Some country fans might hate me. The devil definitely hates me and will do everything he can to stop me. But I remembered that Jesus said in John 16:33, "Take heart! I have overcome the world." He has already overcome the world and the Evil One. So I'll keep my life hidden in His.

I know I will face trials and tribulations of all kinds. I know I'll face temptations and persecution. I have really hard days sometimes. And I have really amazing days too. I will get to experience the delight of suffering for the One I love. I get to share in His sufferings and His victories.

Jesus stayed true to His mission while He was on the earth—relentlessly true to it. He did not compromise with the world or conform to its systems. And the world hated Him for it. They did not understand Him.

He looked like a rebel because, in many ways, He was one. He walked in direct opposition to the dark culture of this fallen world. He carried light and truth. In fact, it is truer to say He *is* Light and Truth.

My friend, when you walk with Jesus, the Light of the World, you, too, will be seen as a rebel to the darkness in the world. You *will be* a rebel to that darkness and to the lies of the Evil One. Anything less is compromise. Does the thought fill you with excitement? Fear? A little of both? That is natural, and that is okay. As we will discover in the pages of this book, we cannot do this on our own. But through the strength and grace of Christ and the knowledge of who He really is, we can do all things.

I, for one, never want to compromise the gospel of Jesus Christ or water down His truth. If being a rebel is what it takes to be a light to the people walking in darkness, a rebel is what I'll be. Are you with me?

TURNING OUR HEARTS TO JESUS

Jesus,

Thank You for coming for me and for rescuing me from the kingdom of darkness. I am forever grateful that You never gave up and You never gave in. You were a rebel against evil for me, and I want to be willing to be a rebel for You. Please give me the desire and the courage to set aside what others might think of me or what names I might be called so that I can follow in Your footsteps. You laid down Your life so that I can have eternal life. I choose to lay down my life for You so that You can live Your life through me and I can share Your love with the world.

Amen.

CHAPTER 2

FOLLOWING JESUS

I'm going to jump right into the deep end with y'all. Are you ready for it?

Take a deep breath.

When it comes to following Jesus, there can be no gray area about our devotion to Him. Jesus made it pretty clear when He said, "Whoever is not with me is against me, and whoever does not gather with me scatters" (Matthew 12:30). We are either with Him or against Him—nothing in between.

I'm here to propose that a rebel doesn't do this Christian life half-heartedly. We go all in, especially when it comes to following Jesus. The decision to follow Jesus is not meant to be this quiet little moment where we kind of agree to believe in Jesus but then go on living how we always did. It's a sudden turning away from everything in order to follow Him. We turn our back on our sin and our selfishness and go after Jesus with everything we have. We literally change allegiance from one kingdom to another!

Imagine you had an incurable and life-threatening illness and the one person who has the antidote to save your life just walked by you. Wouldn't you drop everything and run after the one who has the cure? That is Jesus, but He doesn't only offer the antidote for a sickness. He has the antidote for death, sin, loneliness, fear, pain, and so much more. The healing He offers will last *forever*!

In return, Jesus wants us to truly follow Him—not just on Sundays or when the pastor is watching. He's after more than our occasional good behavior. He's after our whole heart. And true followers of Jesus let the world know what He has done for them; they shine their light into the darkness of the world around them.

Let's go back to the imagery of a life-saving cure. If you knew about the cure for a deathly illness, would you keep quiet about it? Or would you want to share it with every person infected by that disease? Wouldn't you be so excited to be the one who gets to tell them that they can actually live and not die? We are called to do just that with the good news of Jesus Christ. The world is dying around us, and He is our great cure.

Jesus shares about what it means to be a follower of His in Matthew 10:33, "Whoever denies Me before men, I will also deny him before My Father who is in heaven" (NASB1995). He goes on in the next several verses to say that He came to the world to bring a dividing sword and that families would even be separated over Him. Jesus said that if we love the world or other people more than we love Him, we are not worthy of Him: "The one who does not take his cross and follow after Me is not worthy of Me" (v. 38 NASB).

Jesus speaks some hard words here. These are not the words of a weak man. These are not the words of a passive leader who just wants us all to play nice. These words are spoken by a Warrior who is calling us to risk it all for a greater reward. This is an ultimatum, spoken by a fierce and determined King. He draws a line in the sand—are we with Him or are we not? He wants our whole heart. It's all or nothing.

Notice the word *follow* from that passage above. It is crucial that we get this part. Jesus does not ask us to go it alone, nor does He require what He has not already given. He's not a tyrant who places pointless demands for the sake of an ego-fueled power trip. Oh no, that is not my Jesus. He first came for us, willing to give up His life for us. The Maker of All laid aside His divinity and entered the world He created. He became a man so that He could set all humankind free! We were slaves to the Evil One, and Jesus came to rescue us.

You guys, can you wrap your heart and mind around this? This is better than any fairy tale ever written. Our Hero God came to our rescue! He broke down every wall, kicked in every door, and led His bride to freedom. That means you! With fierce love in His eyes, He rushes into your prison cell and says to you, "Follow Me!" Follow Him to freedom, to forgiveness, to healing, to love, and to *life*! He gave His all for you. And all that He asks in return is everything.

FOLLOW ME

At the beginning of His three-year mission on earth, Jesus chose twelve Jewish men to walk by His side. They were from various walks of life, but all had one major thing in common: When Jesus said, "Follow Me," they immediately dropped everything and followed Him anywhere and everywhere. Here is an example from Scripture:

> As Jesus was walking by the Sea of Galilee, He saw two brothers, Simon who was called Peter, and Andrew his brother, casting a net into the sea; for they were fishermen. And He said to them, "Follow Me, and I will make you fishers of men." Immediately they left their nets and followed Him. Going on from there He saw two other brothers, James the son of Zebedee, and John his brother, in the boat with Zebedee their father, mending their nets; and He called them. Immediately they left the boat and their father, and followed Him. (Matthew 4:18–22 NASB1995)

Try to imagine this moment: the look in Jesus' eyes, the sound of His voice. The call was simple and unexpected. One minute they were fishing; the next they dropped everything to follow a man they had never met. *Follow Me*. How His words must have exploded in their spirits! These were not mere words. This was the call of God. And they answered immediately. They left their careers, their homes, their reputations, and their families. Everything. Little did they know at the time, but they would eventually give up their very lives for the One they followed. It was all a small price to pay for the honor of walking with Jesus and gaining an eternity of love, joy, laughter, and peace, which is exactly what Jesus died to give us—eternal life!

"My sheep listen to My voice; I know them, and they follow me. I give them eternal life, and they shall never perish; no one will snatch them out of My hand" (John 10:27–28).

THE DUST OF MY RABBI

When I was a teen, I remember going to my mentor Erica's church one Sunday to hear her share a teaching on following Jesus. She talked about how Jewish disciples who followed a rabbi (a Jewish religious teacher) were meant to follow in the footsteps of their rabbi in every respect. They were to imitate him, memorize his teachings, and apply the lessons to their lives. It is said that their goal was to walk so closely behind the rabbi that the dust his feet kicked up on the dry roads would literally cover them. Following closely meant being covered in the dust of their rabbi.

Jesus was often called Rabbi by His followers. He is our perfect Teacher, and we are meant to follow closely in His footsteps. This means that we imitate Him. We memorize His words. We try to live a life of obedience that proves we are His. Jesus' life was not intended just to be studied but to be imitated. He modeled for us how to live a life empowered and directed by God's Holy Spirit. He told His followers that He only did what the Father taught and only said what He heard the Father say (John 12:49–50). That is our standard.

Erica has such a sweet and calming voice. But that day, her words pierced my soul. They called me to a deeper level of discipleship in my walk with God. They lit a fire in me to sit at the feet of Jesus and learn from Him, like His disciples did. I want to follow Him so closely that I'm covered in His dust. And when people look at me, I hope they don't see me as much as they see the evidence of Christ. I want to choose to sit humbly at His feet, to follow closely, to do and say only what He leads me to do and say. What about you? Do you want to be covered in the dust of your Rabbi?

You might be thinking of areas in your life where you are following more closely to someone or something other than to Jesus. Maybe it's a relationship, a job, a sport, or something like fear or self-protection. If you are becoming aware of this right now, that is probably God speaking to you and inviting you to turn away and follow Him. No matter how important that thing is or how scary it feels to lay it down for Jesus, I promise you that it is nothing compared to what you gain with Him.

HEAVENLY PERSPECTIVE

When I chose to follow Jesus as a twelve-year-old girl, He truly changed my life! I felt fully loved and free in ways I had never experienced before. But it wasn't until I lost my brother, Jacob, when I was fifteen that I began to truly comprehend just how great a gift Jesus had given me. Losing Jacob was like losing a part of myself. I faced the greatest pain of my life following his death, and it threatened to destroy me and my faith. I had to make a decision to believe that God is good—even in the midst of that terrible loss. He did not stop Jacob's death, and I could not understand why. Right from the initial shock, God asked me if I would trust Him in it. I said yes. And I clung to the words of Job: "The Lord gave and the Lord has taken away. Blessed be the name of the Lord" (1:21 NASB). (If you would like to know more about that journey of grief and healing, I share all about it in my first book, *My Jesus*.)

When my brother, Jacob, left this earth suddenly late one summer night, he went straight to the arms of Jesus. And so did a piece of my heart. I was forever changed from that moment on. Some of those changes are obvious: Jacob will never again join our family this side of heaven, and I will miss him with every breath I take. I carry a pain and a longing within me that will never leave until I see him again. But his death also changed my perspective on life. Knowing that Jacob is with Jesus and that I *will* see him again one day fills my heart with joy and comfort, even on the hardest of days. There is more though. I have gained an eternal perspective. Like I said, part of my heart is already in heaven. I now look at life knowing that this earth is not our final destination. This earth does not hold our true reward. What we do here matters in eternity, but this temporary world is not our home. Heaven is.

As excruciating as it has been to lose Jacob here on earth, it has also helped set me free to take a bolder stand for Jesus. Whenever I am tempted to compromise my message or give up altogether, I think of Jacob. He's already there with Jesus, cheering me on as I run my race. I remind myself that heaven is my home and in that coming kingdom is where I will receive my reward, like Jacob already has.

Maybe you, too, have a loved one cheering you on from heaven, and you can deeply relate to what I'm saying here. If so, I am truly sorry for the pain of your loss because I know what you have walked through. But even if you have not faced a deep loss like that, you can still choose to keep your heart set on what really matters. God sees everything, every public moment and every private struggle. When you get to heaven, it will all be revealed. Everything will be made right. You can endure better here on earth when you *know* at a deep level that your true home awaits, where all things will be made new.

Whatever you are facing—God knows, He sees, and He cares. He walks with you through every struggle in this life, loving you perfectly and encouraging you with His words, "Follow Me." It's an invitation not only into salvation but also into the deep things of God, into healing, into growth that you can't even fathom yet. It's an invitation into real life. He's inviting you into an incredible journey where you will be tried and tested, but you will also see miracles happen and lives changed, including your own. Are you ready to live your own fairy tale and follow the One who rescued you, wherever He leads you? Let's go.

TURNING OUR HEARTS TO JESUS

Dear Jesus,

I hear Your invitation to follow You, and deep inside my spirit says yes. I'm also scared to fully trust and surrender everything. [Take a moment and tell Jesus exactly what holds you back—we all have something.] But I choose now to believe that You are good and that I can trust You with my whole life. I ask for courage and strength to surrender it all and follow You, my Rabbi and my Savior, wherever You may lead. I know this is a choice I will make every day of my life. And right now, today, I choose You because You chose me.

Thank You, God.

Amen.

CHAPTER 3

A REBEL STANDS FOR TRUTH

In early April 2024, right before my album *REBEL* was set to be released, I had the opportunity to play at a country music festival in Ft. Lauderdale, Florida. It was called Tortuga Music Festival, and it was my first country festival since signing with Universal. I had just finished a tour with Scotty McCreery, and I was excited to get a chance to be part of another country music festival. I felt especially honored to headline a small tent. But the day did not go as I had hoped. I was fighting a bad sickness that day and barely had a voice left to sing. I was also battling a lot of negative emotions.

I was overwhelmed by a sense of discouragement every time I peeked out from backstage. The tent was nearly empty, and my start time was drawing too close for comfort. Best known in the Christian music world, I was not yet well known as a country artist. Now no one was showing up to hear me sing this country venue! Did I just throw years of hard work in the music industry down the drain? I'd been killing myself day in and day out for the last three years, and I could not handle the thought that it might all be for nothing. But the empty tent didn't lie. I had sold out my tours in the Christian world—but now I couldn't fill a small tent. What if I had made a mistake by focusing on developing as a country artist?

I wish I could tell you I handled it all with grace and peace and was ready to do my show no matter what. But that's not true. I was a nervous wreck and was battling intense fear that I was going to embarrass myself that day. It's sad to say, but it is just the truth. I did not fit in there, and evidently, everybody knew it. Most of the fans at this festival were barely clothed and deep into partying by this point. How could I relate to them or even get my message across? What in the world was I doing there?

Thank God for family and friends. I could tell my

mom was worried for me. She and my dad spoke truth to me, as they always do, and reminded me of my calling. If God had brought me here, they said, He would give me what I needed, just like He'd done before. In fact, we've seen Him do it over and over. But I was still struggling.

Then, thirty minutes before showtime, Lainey Wilson came to find me. She wanted to tell me how proud she was of me and to encourage me before I went onstage. I confided in Lainey about what was really going on. "Lainey, I'm so nervous! My voice is almost gone, and no one is here for my performance. Plus—I feel like I don't fit in in this world." She had just the right words for me as she reminded me to be my authentic self, which would always be more than enough. That's all I needed to do, she said.

The encouragement from my parents and Lainey helped strengthen my determination to step out onto that stage. I decided that even if my show touched only one person that day, it would be worth it.

Minutes before walking out onstage, I heard a growing buzz of voices. When I pulled the curtain back an inch to look out, I could hardly believe how many people were filling the tent. From old to young and from all walks of life, people were coming. I saw young girls, I saw people who were my typical fans, I saw drunk people who were looking for another fun performance, and I saw many who would never normally attend one of my shows. All coming to hear me sing.

Right before I went out, I stopped to pray. *Lord, I know You called me here. Please give me a passion to do what You have called me to do, and give me Your heart for these people. When I leave the stage, let it be You they are thinking about, not me.* Then I walked out, stood on that stage, and shared Jesus with every person who showed up.

That show was incredible. I started with upbeat songs that have a lighter message and slowly transitioned to the songs with deeper meaning and eventually to sharing my faith. I could feel the Holy Spirit working in that tent. There was a tangible shift in the atmosphere. Some people quickly figured out that this was not where they wanted to be and made their way out of the tent. But others stayed, and I could see an intent look on many of their faces. I saw couples holding hands and crying, many people weeping, and little girls singing along to my songs. There were even people with a beer can in hand, tears on their faces, singing along to "My Jesus." God was touching hearts regardless of how they had walked into that tent—even through the haze of partying and alcohol. I was blown away.

I don't know what all God did in the hearts of the people who heard my story that day, but I do know that none of it would have happened if I hadn't been willing to take a bold stand and proclaim the name of Jesus in a crowd I was not accustomed to. I had ventured outside the comfort of the Christian music world to minister to people who desperately needed to hear the message of truth I carried. It wasn't easy for me to work past the discouragement and fear, but it was so worth it! The worthiest endeavors of life are rarely, if ever, easy.

As I stepped offstage that night, I knew I had obeyed the Lord. And I was confident that I could trust Him with the results. I had planted the seed of truth and God would see to the growth. And guess what? Some of those people who might not normally come to my concerts ended up visiting me out on the Rebel Tour! What an honor to see them again and to know that God was moving in their lives. He had called me, provided the opportunity, provided the encouragement I needed when I was scared, and done the work in the hearts of His people. *He* did it! My part was to follow Him, to stand, and to speak the truth.

STANDING FOR TRUTH

Standing for truth is becoming more and more likely to get you branded as a rebel in our crazy world. Sadly, many people don't even believe in truth, or if they do, they see it as a relative term. *You have your truth and I have mine*, they think. *Do whatever you want, as long as it makes you happy*. But I know that truth is an absolute that never changes, no matter what the world does or thinks. Truth is truth, and it does not change based on how I feel or how anyone else feels. I have built my life on this truth—on Jesus. He said, "I am the way and the truth and the life. No one comes to the Father except through me" (John 14:6). No beating around the bush here. Jesus makes it very clear that He is the only Way. If we want to know truth, we'll find it in Jesus.

I am so saddened, and even frustrated, when I see Christians willing to water down the truth so that the world will accept them or like them a little bit more. I understand how tempting this is. Truly I do. Sometimes I'm faced with the temptation to make my message easier to digest and a little more politically correct so more people in the world will accept me. I have been tempted to change a set list so that my songs aren't so "in your face" about Jesus. I know that if I made just one inappropriate video, I would gain thousands of followers on social media. But would it be worth it? Is that what Jesus would do? Not on your life.

Jesus never watered down the truth or compromised His mission, even when the truth offended people. Want a few examples? I thought you might.

- Jesus told religious leaders how hypocritical they were, in no uncertain terms. He even called them vipers! (Matthew 3:7; 12:34; 23:33)
- He told people they had to be willing to give up everything to follow Him. (Matthew 19:21)
- According to Jesus, we are supposed to forgive and bless our enemies. Ouch. (Matthew 5:44–48; Luke 6:27–28)
- We are to forgive over and over and over again. (Matthew 6:14–15; 18:21–22; Luke 6:37; 23:34)
- If someone demands something of us, we should give even more than they demanded. (Matthew 5:42; Luke 6:30–35)
- We must die to ourselves in order to find true life in Him. (Luke 9:23)
- He said that He is the *only* way into the kingdom of heaven and eternal life. (John 14:6)
- Jesus even said that He would rather we be hot or cold in our faith, and that He will *spit us out of His mouth* if we are lukewarm! (Revelation 3:15–16)

I could go on and on, but you get the picture. When you read Jesus' words in the New Testament, you will see over and over how He spoke truth that astounded His listeners. He spoke as One with authority. He did not worry about what people would think of Him or how it might offend them. He took a clear stand, and He didn't back down.

Now, before you run out the door to start telling people that they are vipers or lukewarm believers, you need to understand another critical part of who Jesus is. He is love. First John 4:7–8 says, "Dear friends, let us love one another, for love comes from God. Everyone who loves has been born of God and knows God. Whoever does not love does not know God, because *God is love*." Jesus had perfect love for every person He encountered, even the ones He spoke a hard truth to. Sometimes, true love says the hard thing that no one else is willing to say. He loves us so well that He is willing to offend and even make us angry so we can hear His truth and be set free (John 8:32).

As we take a bold stand for Jesus and speak truth to a lost world, we must be sure we are operating out of God's love. It's God's love that sent Jesus to the cross to die for our sins (1 John 4:9–10), and love motivates Him to expose the lies we believe. If we are truly following

Him, we, too, will speak truth in love. Ephesians 4:15 says, "Speaking the truth in love, we will grow to become in every respect the mature body of him who is the head, that is, Christ."

Here's a question for you: If you speak truth in love, will you ever offend people? The short answer is, yes. How do I know? Well, Jesus is Truth and He is Love. Yet He offended people quite often. To the point that they killed Him—not by some secret hit job but through a public hanging on a cross *after* they had beaten Him to a pulp.

You might be thinking, *Yeah, but those were His enemies. Surely He didn't offend those close to Him.* Think again, my friend. Let's look at what Jesus said to one of His closest friends and followers, the disciple Peter. Jesus had been explaining to His inner circle that He must go to Jerusalem, suffer at the hands of the religious leaders, be killed, and then be raised back to life. But Peter could not accept it.

"Peter took Him aside and began to rebuke Him. 'Never, Lord!' he said. 'This shall never happen to you!' Jesus turned and said to Peter, 'Get behind Me, Satan! You are a stumbling block to me; you do not have in mind the concerns of God, but merely human concerns'" (Matthew 16:22–23).

Can we all just let that sink in for a moment? Jesus called Peter "Satan" and told him he was being a stumbling block! You cannot convince me that this wasn't offensive to Peter. Would you be offended by that? Me too. I would have dissolved into tears, truth be told. Why did Jesus say this? I believe He was making it very clear that this type of self-protective thinking was not of God. The origin of this thinking was from Satan, and self-protection was a stumbling block to Jesus and His mission. He came to lay down His life for His people, not protect Himself from the very purpose of His ministry.

I think the last sentence Jesus said in that passage is extremely important. He exposed how Peter was thinking about human concerns, not the things that concerned God. This is true of us all at times, isn't it? We get so focused on ourselves and our temporary human matters that we forget the bigger picture. We lose our eternal perspective. We protect ourselves and the little world we've created around us. I think oftentimes we get most offended when we are most focused on ourselves. If Peter had understood and been focused on Jesus' true mission, he never would have said what he did.

But Peter did say those words, and Jesus did not let it slide. His rebuke was sharp yet true. It was more important to Jesus that Peter snap out of it, so to speak, than it was to protect Peter's feelings or his ego. Peter had given in to the deceptive thoughts of the Enemy, but Jesus cut right to the heart of the matter and set Peter free with His words—true but painful words. As the writer of Hebrews affirmed, "The word of God is alive and active. Sharper than any double-edged sword, it penetrates even to the dividing of soul and spirit, joints and marrow; it judges the thoughts and attitudes of the heart" (4:12).

Jesus loves us and cares about our feelings. He created them, for crying out loud. But He would never let us stay enslaved to lies or sin just to spare our feelings. He is willing to offend our fragile egos to save our eternal souls. Jesus does what we all should do—He keeps feelings and emotions in their rightful place, and that is in submission to the truth.

CHOOSING TO STAND

I had some opportunities during the 2024 election to either take a stand or stay quiet. If you follow me on social media at all, you already know that I decided to take a stand. Mind you, I didn't take a stand for politics or politicians. Even though what I stood up for was truth and life, these issues often play out in the political realm. God exists in a reality far above the rulers and kingdoms of this world, yet He does involve Himself in our world's systems for His perfect purposes. We see this many places in Scripture, including in Daniel 2:21: "He [God] changes times and seasons; he deposes kings and raises up others. He gives wisdom to the wise and knowledge to the discerning."

It is my belief that as Christians we are to stand for the truth of God in every arena of our lives, from personal to public to political. Whether we are playing sports, country music shows, or the stock market, we must let our light shine for Jesus. Whether we are in the grocery store or in Congress, we bring God's kingdom with us everywhere we go. It is our job to speak up for the afflicted, the downcast, the orphans, the widows, the weak, and the wounded. Jesus is the truth. Let me challenge you with this thought: If we are too afraid to speak up for truth to the world around us, doesn't that mean we are afraid to speak up for Jesus? Are we too worried about upsetting the people around us to say what needs to be said? Are we afraid to offend and therefore we stay silent in the face of evil and lies?

I do not want those words to be true of me. I have chosen to speak up for unborn life and for the truth about how God created humanity: a man and a woman who chose to turn away from God and a Savior who came to win us back again. I have chosen to stand on the Word of God in my decision-making for my career. I've chosen to share the gospel of Jesus Christ with every audience I sing to. I have chosen to pray for my leaders, both the ones I agree with and the ones I disagree with. And I want to encourage you to do the same and to pray for all elected officials, that God will touch their hearts and give them wisdom. These thoughts and desires are what motivated me to write the song "Stand" in 2024. I know the Holy Spirit inspired these words in my heart, and I hope they encourage and inspire you as well:

Stand for injustice, stand for the weak
Stand for the voiceless that need you to speak
Stand for what's right, stand for what's true
Stand like a cross on a hill that stood for you
Stand, stand your ground
Say, "I won't back down even when
my whole world's against me
I'm standing strong 'cause I know who's with me"

CHALLENGING CULTURAL NORMS

When we choose to stand for truth and to carry the kingdom of God with us everywhere we go, we will be in direct opposition to the Enemy's systems in this world. A rebel for Jesus challenges the trends that have become normal in our culture yet are contrary to God's kingdom. We don't just follow the crowd and believe every lie fed to us. A Jesus rebel will test everything against the Word of God and then take a stand for what is right. We ask ourselves: *Am I honoring God in all that I do and say?*

I know from experience that you can't do this in your own strength. It can be scary and even painful to challenge the cultural norms of this world. Many people will resist or even ridicule you. The Enemy will definitely try to stop you. Don't let that keep you from doing the right thing.

In my life, I've taken a stand about how I dress. In the music industry, women are often sexualized. There have been times when I felt pressure to wear more revealing clothing. But I put my foot down and said no. I want to be respected for the message I share, not for how my body looks. Revealing outfits and inappropriate lyrics tend to draw likes and follows, but I'm not looking for that kind of attention. The only reason I am walking this path is to share about my Jesus and bring Him glory.

I really mean it when I pray for people to be thinking of Jesus, not me, when they leave my concerts. This affects every decision I make about how I dress and how I present myself. I do not want to draw unhealthy attention to myself or to dishonor my own body, which is the temple of God. He lives inside me. When I started doing country music festivals, people sometimes reacted in shock to my outfits, saying, "Wow. You're clothed!" making the situation a bit awkward. Maybe I stood out like a sore thumb, but in the end, I believe people respected me for my decision, maybe more so than if I had gone along with the crowd. I have a strong conviction from the Lord to honor Him with how I dress, even if it's not popular today.

Modesty can be a touchy and confusing subject. What is acceptable in one culture is not in another. What you wear to the beach you would never wear to work. What we wear now people never would have worn a hundred years ago. So how do we know what is right? Well, Jesus always brought everything back to the motives of our heart, and we should too. Ask yourself, *What is going on at the heart level?* I have to ask myself questions like: *Am I trying to draw attention to myself in how I dress? Does my outfit distract people from focusing on Jesus? Am I trying to fit in or to honor God?* You can do the same in any area of your life. If what you are doing is intended to bring yourself attention and praise, you need to surrender it to Jesus. A Jesus rebel will stand out in the right ways, ways that bring God the glory.

Whether it is the realm of modesty, social media usage, inappropriate language, what shows we watch, refusing drugs and alcohol, choosing not to believe everything the media tells us, or any other "normal" cultural trend, going against the flow takes courage. If I relied only on my own bravery to do it, I'd fall flat faster than you can say giddyup! I have to keep my heart well grounded in the Word and in the strength God gives me to avoid the temptations that come my way. Just like you, I feel the pull to blur the lines so I'll be liked or admired. I struggle with thoughts of taking the easy way out to avoid painful rejection. I get bombarded with lies from the Enemy that encourage me to do what brings me comfort because I "deserve" this, that, or the other. Only by the power of God through His Holy Spirit can you and I resist the onslaught of the Enemy, in public and in private moments.

I do not want to claim one thing onstage and then do the opposite in private. I want to walk worthy of my Lord every moment of the day. On my own, it's impossible. But with Christ, you and I can walk this out! I often declare these words of the apostle Paul over my life: "I have been crucified with Christ; and it is no longer I who live, but Christ lives in me; and the life which I now live in the flesh I live by faith in the Son of God, who loved me and gave Himself up for me" (Galatians 2:20 NASB).

The pressure from the world to fit in is not going to stop anytime soon. But we have a secret weapon. Jesus has already overcome the world, and we belong to Him! Take a moment to meditate on His words in John 16:33: "These things I have spoken to you so that in Me you may have peace. In the world you have tribulation, but take courage; I have overcome the world" (NASB).

We need the courage and peace that come only from Jesus to truly take a stand in this world. He gives it. Our job is to believe and to receive. But there is another critical component, and it's all about your identity. I'm going to talk in more depth about this in the next chapter, but let me hit a key point here. If I didn't know who I am in Christ and that He loves me with perfect love, I know I would give in to the worldly pressure to get attention through revealing clothing or suggestive videos. We all have a God-given desire deep inside for attention and love. This is a good thing. It should draw us to God. But when we aren't filling that desire with the attention and love of God, we will inevitably look for attention and love from other places. And we won't be able to stand against the tide of ungodly cultural norms.

STANDING ON THE WORD OF GOD

I do not claim to have all the answers about how to stand for Christ in this world. Admittedly I haven't had to face severe persecution or life-and-death ultimatums for the name of Jesus. Yet. But I want to be ready if the time comes. I want to be willing to lay it all down or face persecution for Him, to follow in the footsteps of all the martyrs and members of the persecuted church around the world who have gone before us. They are the true heroes of the faith. I can't fathom the reward they will receive when they enter God's presence in heaven. I try to imagine the moment they meet Jesus face-to-face, but it's too beautiful for words.

I will, however, share with you the best advice I have right now, from my own experience and from the Word of God. First, decide to be a wholehearted follower of Jesus. Make a choice to give your whole heart and whole life to Christ, not just in part. Don't be half-hearted or lukewarm. Be all in. All of us are going to bet our lives on something—let it be on Jesus. Once you decide this and surrender to Him, life gets so much more beautiful. Follow Him with abandon like the disciples did. As you learn about and grow closer to the heart of God, your own heart will shift until you want what He wants. And then nothing will matter more to you than pleasing Him, the One who loves you best. With every decision you make to stand for truth, the next one will be easier.

Second, stand on the Word of God, the holy Scriptures. Read the accounts of His followers in the Bible. Read Jesus' own words of life and truth. Build up your own faith by learning about the faith of others and the love of God. Learn what your identity is in Christ! Most important, in order to share and stand on truth, it is vital that you *know* what the truth is! How can we declare what we do not know? And when the attacks of the world come, the Word of God is your weapon. Ephesians tells us that part of our armor as Christians is "the sword of the Spirit, which is the word of God" (6:17). We cannot go out into this world unarmed.

You will be faced with these battles every day until you go home to heaven. You are in this world to know and become more like Jesus and to tell others about Him. But this world is not your home. We, as Jesus followers, should not look like the world looks, talk like the world talks, or act like it acts. We should look like Him. Challenge the norms of this world. We are part of the kingdom of God now, and that means being a rebel—taking a stand for truth.

TURNING OUR HEARTS TO JESUS

Jesus prayed this prayer for His disciples in John 17:15–18: "I do not ask You to take them out of the world, but to keep them from the evil one. They are not of the world, even as I am not of the world. Sanctify them in the truth; Your word is truth. As You sent Me into the world, I also have sent them into the world" (NASB1995).

Sit with this a moment, and then pray it over yourself back to God.

> *God, I'm not asking You to take me out of this world but to keep me from the Evil One. I am not of this world, just like You are not of this world. Sanctify me in the truth; Your Word is truth. As*

You sent Jesus into the world, Jesus has sent me. Help me receive Your peace and the courage to bring light to the darkness and hope to the hopeless. Ground me in who I am in You. Help me stand firmly on the Rock of my salvation, Jesus Christ.
Amen.

CHAPTER 4

A REBEL'S IDENTITY

Back in 2020, I walked into a songwriting session feeling insecure and somewhat fragile inside. Do you know the feeling? In the days and weeks leading up to this session, I had been in my head, comparing myself to other girls, and I kept coming up short. I looked at their beauty, their success, their fun and exciting lives . . . and compared it all to what I deemed my weakest areas. I didn't feel pretty enough, strong enough, or confident enough. My mind kept circling the same thoughts, questions, and insecurities and coming to the same final conclusion: I'm not enough.

I was supposed to be writing a song with Matthew West and Jeff Pardo that day, the men I had written

"My Jesus" with just days before. Coming off a writing day like that one, when I experienced God inspire such a life-changing song for me, you'd think I would feel confident and secure in His love. I should have been hopeful and expectant about what God would do. But I was losing the battle in my mind. Comparison had snuck in and stolen my confidence, my joy, and my gratitude. Comparison had me focused on myself instead of on Jesus.

I'm not sure why I chose vulnerability that day. I can only assume it was by the leading of the Holy Spirit. Instead of bottling up my struggle and pretending to be strong (which is a constant temptation), I decided to share with Matthew and Jeff what was actually going on inside me. I told them about the comparison struggle in my mind and how it was making me feel so down on myself. They suggested that we flip this attack on its head and write a song about my identity in Christ. Brilliant. Instead of focusing on the lies that were filling my mind, we focused on who I am in Christ and started brainstorming lyrics. Some of the best songs come from a broken place. That is exactly what happened that day, when we wrote "Hey Girl."

Many people probably think I wrote that song for other young ladies who need to know who they are in

Christ. But in reality, I wrote it for myself. I was the one who needed the message of truth that "Hey Girl" carries. And I need it still. What is so beautiful about this song and the way it came about is that, out of my vulnerability and struggle, God has used this song to speak to thousands of young girls about who they are in Christ. In a world that overwhelms us with false messages about our identity, this song proclaims the truth of our worth in Christ.

I'm a blood bought, battle fought, all my shame long gone
Made new child of the King
I'm an amen, testify, holy water baptized
Went down and came up clean.

From the day we put those lyrics on paper to this very day, every time I sing the words of "Hey Girl," I am reminded of how God sees me. He decided I was worth His sacrifice and suffering. He chose me and He made me new, washing away all my sin and shame. Every feeling of inadequacy or of not measuring up to others pales in comparison to the realization that Jesus gave *everything* . . . for me. He determined the value of my life and was willing to pay the highest price of all to buy me back from the Evil One. And the exact same is true of you.

When you meditate on this truth and let it truly settle into your soul, everything changes. I encourage you to do this right now. Say (or sing) these lyrics out loud over and over, until they take root in your heart and mind. Sing the truth over yourself.

The song "Hey Girl" was the catalyst for a new part of my ministry as well. Originally we were focusing on the core audience of Christian music: women in their thirties and forties. But after I released "Hey Girl," suddenly little girls and teens started flooding my concerts like never before. They would climb the stairs at the churches where I was singing and dance in the aisles. Precious young ladies showed up in their very own ruffles and sparkly boots to sing with me about Jesus and who He created us to be!

I could sense that God had a plan here that was bigger than one song. We followed His leading, and soon after launched a new platform called Hey Girl Nation, which is a ministry focused on women of all ages finding their identity in Christ. From young to old, we want ladies to come together and encourage one another. We share our stories and our struggles. We highlight God's victories and pray for each other when we're fighting hard battles. Instead of comparison that tears us apart, Hey Girl Nation strives to bring women together as we focus on Jesus.

The song "Hey Girl" had another unexpected blessing for me. But this last one didn't play out for a few years. While writing the album *REBEL*, the truth I had allowed to fill my heart and mind while writing "Hey Girl" gave me the confidence I needed for my new adventure. I was walking into writing sessions with some amazing and well-known people, which can be very intimidating. It was vital that I was rooted in my identity in Christ before ever stepping foot into those rooms, or I wouldn't have been able to remain true to what God had called me to do. I would have given in to comparison and insecurity. Intimidation would have eaten my lunch.

But, once again, God had gone before me. He gave me exactly what I needed to remain steady in new and scary environments. I won't pretend that I don't ever get nervous or fight feelings of intimidation. I still have to battle. But I'm fighting *from* a place of victory, not for victory. Jesus already won the battle, and He is the Rock I am standing on. I put my life in His hands at the age of twelve. He helped me solidify my identity in Him further in 2020. And every day of my life, I do my best to place my life in His hands before stepping into whatever that day holds. And He's already won your battle too, my friend. He's inviting you deeper into knowing your full identity in Him.

A DEEP LONGING

Deep inside, each and every one of us longs to be loved and wanted. We need to belong. We crave acceptance. These aren't desires we should try to extinguish. God put these longings inside of us to lead us to Himself. Our real need is the love, acceptance, and belonging we find in God. There is a part of us that will never be satisfied without Him. We are meant to be accepted. We were created to belong. God is love, and when we find ourselves in Him, we experience perfect love. God has adopted us as His children. We are His. Forever.

> See what great love the Father has lavished on us, that we should be called children of God! And that is what we are! (1 John 3:1)

Sadly, at some point, we all go looking for acceptance and identity in the wrong places. Here are a few of the areas where the Enemy tempts us to find ourselves outside of Jesus. See if any of these strike a chord in you:

- Appearance and beauty
- Expensive or trendy clothing and shoes
- Intelligence

- Athleticism, strength, and physical fitness
- Having a "good" reputation
- Being a "nice" and likable person
- Religious self-righteousness (trying to be good all on our own and the pride that comes with that)
- Popularity and fame
- Online popularity with followers, comments, and likes
- The foods we eat or don't eat
- The clique or club we're accepted into
- Money
- Success
- Power and control—the need to be in charge
- Illness or disability
- Who we love and who loves us
- What we drive
- Our family

I imagine you could add many more items to that list. Sadly, the number of ways we can try to find our identity outside of God is almost endless. Satan has made sure of that. But no matter how many temptations we face to find acceptance and worth in the world, there is only one true Source. It's Jesus, the One who proved you were worth everything to Him, the God of the universe who was willing to lay down His own life to save you and buy you back from the kingdom of darkness. When the Bible says Jesus has redeemed us or provided our redemption, it means He has paid a price to cover the debt we owe! The price He paid for me and for you is His very own life. There is no higher price than Jesus Himself. You are a blood-bought, battle-fought, made-new child of the King!

> He has rescued us from the dominion of darkness and brought us into the kingdom of the Son he loves, in whom we have redemption, the forgiveness of sins. (Colossians 1:13–14)

The temptation to let the world define you won't stop coming. This is not something you face once and then it's over. Every day of your life, you will have to choose to center yourself in God and let Him remind you who you are. Every time you're scared, hurting, or lonely, you get to decide if you will look for relief and acceptance in the things of this world or if you will rebel against the world's lies and temptations and run into the arms of the Father. Suit up, warrior, you are in a battle for your soul.

I face these decisions all the time, just like you do. Will I compromise my message to gain followers, or will

I stay true no matter what happens? Will I allow the music industry to shape me with its formulas for success, or will I allow God to determine my steps and trust the results to Him? Will I cave to intimidation and change myself so others approve of me, or will I stand firm in my identity in Christ? Will I compare myself to other women, hoping I'll somehow measure up, or will I trust that God made me just the way I am for a purpose and is well pleased with His creation? Where will my heart run when my identity is threatened? Will I cave to the pressure, or will I be a rebel against the ways of the world? Does any of this sound familiar to you?

NO COMPARISON

Early on in my career, while we were creating the first album, some people in the industry tried to convince me to change my voice. You see, I have a natural vibrato that is very fast. Vibrato is that subtle (or sometimes not-so-subtle) pulsating of a singer's voice. You might hear a very strong vibrato in an opera singer's voice but none at all in the pure tone of a young child singing in the choir. Well, I have a natural vibrato that is quite noticeable and quick. Some people around me at the time felt that I should work to reduce and even eliminate my vibrato. They feared that Christian radio might not want to play someone with that kind of sound. In this instance, instead of being not enough, I was hearing the message that I was too much. I was being advised to tone down and even change my natural self so I could be accepted.

Since I was so young, it was very tempting to just listen to the people who "knew better" and go along with their advice. They wanted me to succeed, and they thought that was the way to do it. My youth and inexperience left me feeling uncertain. *Should I listen to this advice?* I took my questions to the Lord. I talked to my family. And ultimately, God sent someone to speak exactly what I needed to hear.

I spent some time working with an award-winning songwriter and producer. And I learned that he loved my natural vibrato. When I told him I was being pressured to get rid of it, he adamantly spoke against that. He told me that this is how God made me. My voice is a God-given gift, and I shouldn't change myself to please people. I was made to sound this way, designed by God Himself!

That was enough for me. But he added the cherry on top when he told me that he has worked with artists who try to develop the kind of vibrato I have, and they can't do it, even after ten years of work! Why would I stop using such a precious and unique gift? I decided then and there that I would use the voice God gave me and wouldn't try to change it just to fit in or be accepted. I turned from comparison and insecurity to gratitude for this amazing gift from God. And I stood my ground.

Whether the world tries to tell you that you aren't enough or you're too much, those statements are all lies. Comparing yourself to others will never lead to truth, joy, or freedom. Instead, it will enslave you to trying to live up to a false reality the world is showing you, and it will steal your joy. You'll never be content trying to be someone other than who God created you to be. God didn't call you to fit some cookie-cutter version of another human or to be like everyone else. He created you unlike any other person who has ever lived or will ever live. And He loves what He made in you. No one else carries exactly what you carry. Please don't hide the gifts God has given you just so other people might accept you. That would be a tragedy.

Take a moment to consider the following words of David as he described how lovingly God created each of us. I encourage you to let these be more than just words. Sit with this for a moment, and let the Holy Spirit settle this truth in your heart:

For you created my inmost being;
you knit me together in my mother's womb.
I praise you because I am fearfully and wonderfully made;
your works are wonderful,
I know that full well.
My frame was not hidden from you
when I was made in the secret place,
when I was woven together in the depths of the earth.
Your eyes saw my unformed body;
all the days ordained for me were written in your book
before one of them came to be. (Psalm 139:13–16)

For quite a few years now, I have taken time at the start of each new year to ask the Lord for a word for the upcoming year. I follow the plan John Eldredge lays out for setting aside time to listen to the Lord and receive a word from Him that will define my year in some important way.[1] In the moment, I may not always understand the fullness of what the word will mean to me in the coming year. But I receive and meditate on it, knowing that God is being very intentional with me.

Usually I hear one singular word from God, but in 2024, something new happened. Instead of a word, I heard a scripture reference: 2 Corinthians 10:12. I had no idea what that Bible verse talks about, and I didn't hear anything else. So after a moment of wondering, I grabbed my Bible to see what God was telling me. When I turned to that verse, I read these words: "We do not dare to classify or compare ourselves with some who commend themselves. When they measure themselves by themselves and compare themselves with themselves, they are not wise." Whoa. That could not be more clear. Whatever I was going to face in 2024 would require that I not compare myself with others. It's foolish to do so.

It didn't take long for me to see why God had given me that verse as my "word" for 2024. That year, I walked into writing sessions with well-known and extremely talented artists. I opened for country stars who are way more famous than I am and who put on incredible shows. Many of these artists live a very different life than I do, and I often feel out of place. It can be intimidating to say the least. The temptation to compare myself to them is powerful. But once again, God gave me what I needed when I needed it. I stood on that word the entire year, and I still do. I remind myself of all the lessons God has taught me about finding my true identity and worth in Him and not comparing myself to others. It's a daily battle, my friends, and it's often a hard one. But God is in it with us. We are never alone. His Word is the rock we stand on. It's the rock I stand on when I step out onto a stage and feel out of place. He's the One I cling to when the world tells me I'm not enough or I'm too much. I'm not going to try to fit their mold. I'm aiming to look like my Savior.

"WHO DO YOU SAY THAT I AM?"

Maybe it goes without saying, but if we're going to find our identity in God, we really need to know who He is! We really need to *know* Him, on a personal level. It begins when we believe that Jesus is the Son of God, who came to save us from our sins and from death. We receive His forgiveness and His life. Then we follow Him. We learn about Him. We spend time with Him. We listen to what He says and obey. We get to know God on a deep level and let Him transform us into His image. What we behold, we become.

In the early pages of the Bible, you can read about several times when God introduced Himself to His people. In one of these incredible encounters, God met with Moses by a burning bush. God was sending Moses back to Egypt to lead God's people out of captivity and into the promised land. But Moses was scared. First, he essentially asked God, "Why me? Who am I to do this?" Then Moses worried that the people would demand to know who God is. He said to God, "Now they may say to me, 'What is His name?' What shall I say to them?" And God said to Moses "I AM WHO I AM . . . This is what you shall say to the sons of Israel, 'I AM has sent me to you'" (Exodus 3:13–14 NASB).

When asked His own name and identity, God defined Himself *by Himself*. I AM WHO I AM. At first glance, that might seem odd. But let's look closer. God defined Himself by Himself because nothing is greater than Him to use as a way of identity. He basically said, "I AM the One Who Exists." He is the origin of everything. He is the Creator and the Life Force that holds it all together. Everything in the heavens and on earth gets its identity from God, and God is . . . God. Nothing exists outside of The One Who Is.

We usually look to something that is either preexisting or is greater than ourselves for our identity. We use family names, groups of people, careers, nationalities, sports teams, or any number of other identifiers. But God simply said, "I AM WHO I AM." If we follow His example, we will also define ourselves by Him. We will look to the greatest Source of all. We will let the One who created us define our worth and decide our purpose for living. Anything else is a counterfeit identity.

It all begins with knowing who God is. Everything stems from the knowledge of Him. Jesus showed us the way during an encounter with Peter in Matthew 16:13–20. First, Jesus asked His disciples who people in the world were saying He was. His disciples told Him that some people thought He was Elijah, some thought He was John the Baptist, and still others thought He was a prophet of old. Then Jesus took it to a deeper level. He asked them directly, "But what about you? Who do you say I am?" Simon (soon to be called Peter) answered with the truth he could know only by having walked with Jesus and by God's choice to reveal it to him: "Simon Peter answered, 'You are the Messiah, the Son of the living God'" (vv. 15–16).

Jesus' response was to bless Peter and acknowledge that this knowledge could not have come from anywhere else but His Father in heaven. And now the kicker: Peter had his eyes on Jesus. He focused on who God is. Then Jesus turned and told Peter who *he*—Peter—really was. "Jesus replied, 'And I tell you that you are Peter, and on this rock I will build my church, and the gates of Hades will not overcome it'" (v. 18).

Peter did not have to go on some quest to "find himself." He didn't have to join a club, become successful, or try out a thousand different identities. He didn't need to focus on *himself* at all. He followed Jesus; He learned from Jesus; He received the revelation from God of who Jesus really is (not the world's ideas of who He is). And in turn, Jesus gave Peter his true identity! Jesus declared Peter's worth and even gave him a new name.

Do you want to know who you really are? Do you want to know the unique name Jesus calls you? Do you want to know your purpose on this earth? The only way—and I mean *only* way—you will find these answers is by looking to the One who dreamed you up long before you were ever formed in your mother's womb. He planned out all your days before one of them came to be. He knows you inside and out. And He wants you to know Him. It's only when you follow wholeheartedly after Jesus and let Him become the goal of your life that you'll actually find your true self. Isn't that beautifully ironic?

Jesus put it this way: "Whoever wants to be my disciple must deny themselves and take up their cross and follow me. For whoever wants to save their life will lose it, but whoever loses their life for me will find it.

What good will it be for someone to gain the whole world, yet forfeit their soul?" (Matthew 16:24–26).

The world will tell you to find yourself in the systems it has created. It will lie to you that if you focus on yourself, you will find yourself. People will try to get you to fit their own molds. The Enemy wants you lost in *any* identity other than your true one. But you must rebel against all of this. You must stand against the overwhelming tide of lies in this world about who you are and what you're worth. Will you stand with me? Feet planted on the Solid Rock of Jesus Christ, let's lay down our lives, take up our cross, and *follow Him*. Let's lose our lives in Jesus so that we can be found! There is great power in believers who intimately know the One they follow and are walking in their true, God-given identity.

TURNING OUR HEARTS TO JESUS

Creator God,

I believe that You are—and that You are good. I believe that You are the maker of all things, including me. You've made me for a specific purpose and destiny. Please expose the lies I have believed about myself and about You. I ask You to show me who You truly are. And please tell me what my unique identity is in You. Who do You say I am?

Now take some time to listen. You've asked; He'll answer.

CHAPTER 5

A REBEL'S STRENGTH

I was dragging myself across the finish line of a grueling year and coming into 2023 on fumes. I had played 150 shows in 2022 and been away from my home for more than 220 days. It had been incredible and exciting, but it had also been brutal to my soul. As the year drew to a close, I felt like I was carrying the weight of the world on my shoulders. It finally occurred to me that, in some regards, I was.

I am beyond blessed to get to share my story, my songs, and the love of Jesus to crowds of people night after night. Yet the weight of it all was crushing me. I was carrying the burdens of my fans and the pressures of my career with me constantly. I felt responsible for the people I ministered to. Night after night, I met beautiful, broken people and heard their stories of deep grief and amazing rescue. Night after night, I felt that I had a responsibility to help, comfort, encourage, and tend to their hearts. I met people who had just lost a child, needed a miraculous healing, or any number of other deeply grievous situations. I carried their stories and their pain in my heart because I truly do care about each one. I was trying to be strong for them.

Thankfully, the new year brought more than exhaustion. It also brought the sense of a fresh start and some exciting changes into my career. I was stepping into new management, which was a great gift from God. But in that transition, I felt pressure within myself to be put together and to perform at the highest level. I felt that I needed to please everyone around me: fans, management, parents, friends, cowriters, band members, label executives, etc. No one was telling me to perform like this or demanding that I meet all their expectations. It was an internal pressure I had adopted without even realizing what I was doing. I didn't want to let anyone down. It wasn't until the weariness of it all started to catch up with me at the turn of the year that I turned my eyes inward to see what was going on inside. It became obvious that if I didn't sort this out, I wouldn't be able to keep going much longer. My strength was running out.

And on top of the weight I was carrying, my heart was still deep in grief. At that point, Jacob had been gone for five and a half years. I was adjusting to living this life on earth without him, but the pain was still very real and raw. I missed him every single day and ached to hear his voice or feel his hug again. I still do. During every show I performed that year, I would talk from stage about losing Jacob, which both helped me heal and, in some ways, kept the wound fresh and tender. Sharing my story of hope and healing with others who need Jesus' touch is one of the greatest gifts of my life. But it can take a dangerous toll on my heart if I'm not careful.

Telling you this story in a few brief paragraphs makes the issue and solution seem so obvious, but when I was living it, I can assure you that it was not that easy to recognize. I had to nearly hit rock bottom before I came to my senses. When I stop to think about it now, I see how ridiculous it was. I did not create my career—God gave it to me. I did not create my ability to sing or write—God gave it to me. I did not do the work in the hearts and lives of my fans—God did that. So why would I try to carry out His calling for me in my own abilities when

I wasn't the one who started it all in the first place? If I was truly living out a God-sized calling on my life, there was no way I could fulfill it *without* Him! God gives us dreams so incredible—so beyond our own capabilities—that the only way we can reach them is through total reliance on Him. It's not really our works or abilities He's after anyway. He wants our hearts.

It was from this place of deep soul weariness that I stepped into a songwriting session at the start of 2023 with Matthew West and Jeff Pardo. I was beginning to realize what was going on inside me, but I was still struggling with it. I was still carrying a load I couldn't bear and was internally weak to the point of breaking. Thankfully, the Lord has given me cowriters (and friends) like Matthew and Jeff with whom I can be vulnerable. What a relief that I didn't have to go into that writing session pretending to be strong. I could have chosen to pretend that I was okay and that I was strong enough to handle it all. Goodness knows, that's what I'd been doing for months and months. But once again, just like when we wrote "Hey Girl," I decided to just be real with them about my struggle. And once again, Jesus met me there through the honest words of my friends.

"You don't have to pretend like you're strong anymore, Anne," Matthew said. "God's strength is made perfect in your weakness. So if you allow yourself to be vulnerable and weak and you allow yourself to honestly feel these feelings of pressure and anxiety, God is going to meet you in His perfect way. That's where He's going to give you the supernatural strength you need."

I took Matthew at his word because I knew he was speaking God's truth to me. In 2 Corinthians 12:9, the apostle Paul shared what Jesus told him when he was facing a constant battle that was too much for him: "He said to me, 'My grace is sufficient for you, for my power is made perfect in weakness.' Therefore I [Paul] will boast all the more gladly about my weaknesses, so that Christ's power may rest on me."

The song we wrote that day is called "Strong," and it flowed out of that place of weakness and vulnerability. It has become my declaration of reliance upon Jesus and my desperate need for His strength. The lyrics are my personal story, not just sweet-sounding words. "Strong" speaks of putting on a brave face even while on the inside, I may be weary and broken. I didn't know life would be this hard. And it brings me to my knees, calling on the name of Jesus.

Do you find yourself crying out to God in a similar way? Is your soul weary and your heart worn out from trying to carry what only Jesus can? Are you putting on a brave face for the ones you love or for the world around you, yet silently crumbling inside? I encourage you to take a moment with this song and let it sink into the deep parts of your soul. Pray it back to God, admit your areas of weakness, and ask Him to meet you there. He will. He's been waiting for this.

"Dear Lord, Jesus, You know I can't do this on my own."
Lord knows I've tried, but I'm good at falling down
Thank God You're good at picking me up off the ground
The world's gonna try to break me
But I know the One who makes me
Strong

DESPERATE NEED FOR JESUS

The season of writing "Strong" wasn't the first time I've had to face my own inability and weakness in a time of suffering, nor will it be the last. I firmly believe that every experience of pain and suffering in this life is an opportunity for us to see another aspect of God's infinite character. You don't know Him as Healer until you need to be healed. You don't truly experience Him as Comforter until you are grieving and wounded. It's when your resources run dry that He shows up as your Provider. I could go on and on, but you get the point. Each and every time you face hardship, you have the incredible opportunity to experience the goodness of God on a new and personal level. Suffering opens the door to knowing God in a more intimate way. This holds true in our weakness too. Only when we acknowledge our weakness to God can we receive His perfect strength. It's in the weakest moments of our lives that we experience His supernatural strength—because we need it to survive.

As I mentioned before, I will never stop missing Jacob, and the pain of his loss will never fully go away this side of heaven. My brother's death and the years of grief that followed have brought me to the end of my own strength in ways I never could have imagined before I lived it. That place of brokenness and the end of my own strength is exactly where I encountered God in the most life-changing ways. When times are easy, we don't feel the overwhelming need for God. We tend to coast through life in our own strength without even knowing we are doing it. But when our world falls apart, suddenly everything changes.

The initial trauma of losing Jacob had me running to God just to make it through the day—or the hour.

Some days it felt like I needed Him just to help me keep breathing. Day by day, God gave me the strength I needed for the next breath and the next step. As the heartrending trauma gave way to the dull, steady ache of loss and longing, I unknowingly started trying to survive on my own again. I never had the conscious thought that I didn't need God. I knew I was nothing without Him. Yet somehow I felt the internal pressure to be strong for my family. I tried to put on a brave face for those around me.

Do you see the repeated trap I tend to fall into? Part of my personality is that I like helping others. God made me that way, and I love it. But as with everything else in life, if I don't surrender that to God and keep my focus on Him, I will end up trying to do it all by myself. That is not God's intention. My ability to help others will only be effective and godly when it flows from a place of total reliance on the Lord.

What about you? Is there a trap you tend to fall into? Is there a part of your personality that you struggle to keep surrendered to God? Are there ways you are trying to be strong, but you desperately need His help? There's no time like the present. You can talk to Him about it right now.

To this very day, the pain of missing Jacob can still

bring me to my knees in an instant. An unexpected memory hits without warning, and suddenly I can barely breathe. I'm exposed, vulnerable, and wounded. It is very hard to be blindsided with pain that way, but I've come to appreciate the gift of it. The fact that my deep grief for Jacob is a weak spot that can be triggered at any moment keeps me in a place of relying on God's strength. It sends me to my knees or into the fetal position over and over again. The words of my song ring true for this as well. In those moments when I hit my knees, I cry out to my Father that I can't do it on my own. I need Him—right then, right there. Desperately. And He has never ignored that cry. He always shows up, tends to my broken heart, and gives me the strength I need in that moment.

We all have weak spots that can trigger pain or fear in us at a moment's notice. Are you aware of yours? Maybe God is inviting you into a conversation and into deeper healing for that right now. I encourage you not to ignore any prompting in your heart. The Enemy will lie to you and try to tell you that you should not disturb that pain because it will overwhelm you. But nothing can overwhelm Jesus, and He promised never to leave you or forsake you, even (especially) in your pain and your weakness. As you allow the fear or pain to surface, simply keep telling Jesus that you love Him and trust Him there, in the middle of it. And then invite Him into that place with you to speak His truth into it.

DAILY RELIANCE ON GOD

Even though I often wish God would give me an over-abundance of strength so I have enough to keep going for a long stretch, that is not how He tends to operate. Just like God fed the Israelites day by day when they journeyed through the desert, He gives us the grace and strength we need for our current moment. He did not give His people a basketful of food once a week that they could take away and feed themselves with. He did not have a stockpile they could visit whenever they decided it was time. No. Instead, God gave them food each morning (except for the Sabbath, when they rested), which kept them fully reliant on Him on a daily basis. I've seen this same concept proven true in the day-to-day pain and suffering I've experienced since Jacob died and in the pressures of my work. God is my daily bread to keep going, not my weekly, monthly, or yearly bread. Daily.

In the fast-paced and pressure-filled nature of my

music career, it only takes a few days of not spending time with Jesus for me to feel the effects. I probably notice it about the same time that my family and friends can see it too. My personal strength reserves don't last me very long before I become exhausted, worn down, and irritable. When everything starts to drain me and my fuse gets short, it usually means I've neglected my time with Jesus. If I don't put Him first, nothing flows well. But if I take time to center myself in Jesus, worship Him, and receive His strength *before* anything else, I have found that everything just works better. I may not always get the outcome I wanted or expected, but it's always the right outcome if God is in it. He gives me strength for the day, whatever the day may hold. There is so much peace in knowing I can fully rely on Him.

I have had to learn this lesson time and time again. I think that's partly due to the busyness of life and the constant demands I face in my job. What about you? Have you ever felt too busy to spend time with God? Do you jump right to your to-do list and mentally promise to come back to God later? Yeah, me too. But it simply does not pay off in the end. We were not created to do any of this life without God. And He will not bless our attempts to do it on our own, no matter how well-meaning those attempts may be. I'm reminded of the beautiful old hymn that says, "I need Thee, O I need Thee; ev'ry hour I need Thee." It's true. I need Him. Every. Hour.

SELF-RELIANCE: A DANGEROUS PATH

For me personally, burnout and exhaustion are two of the dangers of trying to do life in my own strength. I believe this is true for everyone because we weren't meant to do life on our own. Whether you're a student, an executive, a stay-at-home mom, an electrician, or anything else—God wants you to do all that you do out of relationship with Him. He wants to give you the strength and grace you need, day by day. He wants to give you incredible ideas for your work and strategies that are straight from heaven. He wants you to invite Him into your day and let Him show you the way. He knows that is the safest place for you to be, and He is protecting you from the dangers of trying to make your way through life in your own strength.

The world will try to break you with its lies. It will tell you that you aren't enough, so you may as well just give up and do what makes you happy. Or it will tell you that everything you need is inside you and you don't need anyone else. You should just power through it all alone. Be independent. Pull yourself up by your boot-straps. Man up.

Sound familiar? Remember, the dominion of this world was handed over to Satan by Adam and Eve back in the garden of Eden. Therefore, the systems of this world are not of God. God tells us all throughout the New Testament what His kingdom is like, and it is in direct contrast to the kingdom of this world. If you have accepted His gift of salvation, then you have been rescued from the kingdom of darkness in this world and transferred to His kingdom of light.

When you live according to the culture of the kingdom of God, you will be in rebellion against the systems of this world, which want you focused on yourself. In contrast, God tells us to seek first His kingdom, and then everything else will be added to us (Matthew 6:33). He encourages us to see the kingdom of God like a treasure hidden in a field. When we discover it, we sell everything so we can buy that field (13:44). Nothing should matter more to us than God and the values of His kingdom.

God's kingdom often sounds like a paradox. Jesus says if we want to find our life, we must lose it for His sake (16:25). He says that the first will be last and the last will be first (20:16). He says that the ones who know they are poor in spirit and are nothing without God are blessed and that the kingdom of heaven belongs to them (5:3). He says that when we are weak, then we are strong (2 Corinthians 12:10). Does this sound like the world's system to you? Not even a little bit.

Everywhere you go, you bring the kingdom of God with you. And that's what makes you look like a rebel to this world. So be it. Think of it this way: Whatever your nationality, you carry that with you when you visit foreign countries. I'm an American, and that is pretty obvious when I walk the streets of a European country. Or on a more personal level, you could think of my family. I am Kent Wilson's daughter, and I carry the values he instilled in me everywhere I go. I don't stop being a Wilson when I walk into someone else's home. I bring my identity with me and share the culture of my family. May that be even more true about my heavenly Father. I bear His name and have been transferred to His kingdom. Everywhere I go, I bring the culture and values of the kingdom of God with me. I walk in a strength and authority that is not my own. It's all from Him.

But if we try to go it alone, we are setting ourselves up for trouble. For me, it usually results in reaching the end of my strength and almost (or actually) falling apart.

It's bad for my health and my emotional state. It's hard on me and on those around me. Once I realize I've been walking in my own strength, I have to repent and turn back to God. Thank God, He is always there to pick me up again, forgive me, and give me His strength right in the middle of my weakness.

For some, the danger is falling into the pride of self-reliance. When you think you're doing all these good things on your own, you start to feel proud of your work, your efforts, your right decisions. You start to look down on others who aren't doing what you're doing. And you drift away from God's heart. Listen, we can't even make our hearts beat. We rely on God for our next breath. All things hold together through Christ (Colossians 1:17). If our daily survival depends on God granting us another day of life and breath, how in the world do we think we can actually do *anything* outside His provision and strength? Preposterous.

Or maybe for some, working out of their own strength leads to resentment and bitterness. This can happen when you're helping others and giving outside yourself. You might start out with beautiful motives, but if you continue in your own strength, it can all fall apart when people let you down. And people inevitably will let you down. Maybe your efforts aren't appreciated or your acts of service aren't reciprocated, and if that goes on long enough, you start to grow resentful. It hurts to give and give of yourself and get nothing in return. When we give out of our own strength rather than from the overflow of God's strength within us, we unknowingly set ourselves up for pain and bitterness to take root.

STRENGTH FOR TODAY

It's easy to say we need to rely on God's strength and not our own, but how does that play out on a daily basis? As we already discussed, part of it is seeking God first each day for our strength, our nourishment, our daily bread. I try to get alone with God every day, even if for just a few moments. I like to sneak away with my coffee, Bible, journal, and devotional book. It's easy to do at home, but out on tour, I have to get creative. Sometimes I tuck away in a hidden spot, or I venture out to a local coffee shop. I put on headphones and listen to worship music as I ask God to speak to me. I sip coffee and think about Him. Then I open the Word to see what He has for me, recording it in my journal. I come back to my journal each night to write down at least one thing I am thankful for from the day. It's amazing to see the benefits of ending my day with gratitude. Stress and worries melt away as I turn my heart to Jesus to thank Him for His goodness.

If you don't already, I encourage you to make it a priority to spend time with God each morning before the pressures of life creep in. Choose Him first. Talk to Him, listen to Him, read His Word, submit your day to Him, surrender yourself all over again to God, ask the Holy Spirit to fill you anew, worship God, and thank Him. There's no perfect formula for spending time with God, just like there isn't a formula for going on a wonderful date. Whether you sit down for coffee with God, go on a walk with Him, or find some other special time, seek Him first and get your strength for the day straight from the Source.

It's also important that you slow down enough to realize when you need to pause and recenter in the Lord throughout your day. For me, I will notice feelings of anxiety in my chest, runaway thoughts, or a short fuse. These are all signs that I need to stop and run to Jesus. This doesn't always require an hour of devotional time. It can mean I take one minute and give everything back to God. I recognize that He is my source for everything I need and I choose to receive His strength. I breathe deeply and slowly. I sometimes say out loud, "God, You are real, and You are good. You love me. I can trust You. Thank You for giving me exactly what I need right now." You'll find the words you need to pray when you simply turn your heart to Jesus. There are no magic words, and there is no mathematical formula. It's all about turning to Jesus, choosing Him, and surrendering your life. Again. And again. And again.

God showed me another way to stay rooted in His strength that might be helpful to you too. This happened back in the first few years after losing Jacob. My mentor Erica gave me a necklace with the word *strength* on it. That necklace was a constant physical reminder that God would give me strength to make it through each day. The word *strength* became my theme for that season because I was so dependent on the Lord's strength to survive the pain. It was during this same time that I began to notice surprising little moments of joy. I would find myself smiling and realize that it was a genuine smile, one that started in my chest and reached all the way to my eyes. I didn't have to force it. Laughter would bubble out of me when I was with my friends and would catch me off guard. Wait—was I *allowed* to laugh? At first, I felt guilty for it, until I realized what was happening.

It was the joy of the Lord coming from deep down inside me.

There had been a time when I honestly thought I'd never smile or laugh again. At least not genuinely. When you go through such traumatic pain, it feels impossible that you will ever be happy again. But God is bigger than our pain. And He gives us strength from an unexpected place—His joy. Nehemiah 8:10 says, "The joy of the LORD is your strength." This is not a fleeting happiness based on circumstances. This is a deep-down joy that comes from trusting God. It's a gift. And it flies in the face of our circumstances. It made no sense to feel joy when my heart was so broken. But God's kingdom is different, remember? Just ask the apostle Paul or Corrie ten Boom. They both share amazing stories of finding the joy of the Lord in the midst of the most horrific circumstances. Corrie ten Boom, who faced more grief and loss than most of us ever will, famously said that "joy runs deeper than despair." I'd say she was a beautiful rebel against the ways of this world. She is a hero of mine.

I can tell you from personal experience that the joy of the Lord will give you a supernatural strength no matter what you're facing. It does not disappoint. You will find the greatest peace and joy at the moments of your greatest surrender to God. It happens when we come to the end of ourselves and throw ourselves on His mercy. Give it all to Him, even while you still feel lost at sea.

Choose to trust Him when life still seems out of control. And He will infuse your life with strength, peace, and joy. It's hard to fully describe, but once you experience it, you will know.

God's strength is made perfect in our weakness. It comes from the joy of the Lord in the darkest of times. When we surrender all, we find everything that will ever matter. None of this makes sense to the world. That's why the world will say that you are crazy or delusional or . . . a rebel.

Finally, friends, give God all the glory. I'm going to speak more on this in the next chapter, but it's vital to say here too. Our strength comes from God, and part of staying rooted in His strength is acknowledging that He is your *only* true source. Let your knees hit the ground, raise your hands to the sky, and give thanks and praise to the One who gives you your next breath, the One who makes you strong.

TURNING OUR HEARTS TO JESUS

Dear Lord Jesus,

You know I can't do this on my own. None of it. Not one thing. All my efforts are nothing without You. So I surrender all. I lay it all down at Your feet—everyone and everything in my life. [You might need to spend some time here and name specific things and people you need to surrender to Him.] I am weak and tired. I am weary of trying to power through life on my own. The worries and cares of this life are choking me. I lay it all down.

Please meet me here, in my place of weakness. And over all these situations, over my own heart, I declare that You are real and You are good. You love me eternally, and I can trust You with everything. Your joy is my strength. Give me the joy of the Lord this day and every day. I love You, Jesus. Thank You for Your strength and Your goodness. I rest in You and receive Your perfect strength.

In the mighty name of Jesus, amen.

CHAPTER 6

GIVING GOD ALL THE GLORY

"Anne, your music has changed my life!"

"I couldn't have made it through losing my sister without your book, Anne."

"God is using you to help so many people!"

I'm not going to lie—it feels really good to hear people share such kind words with me. Testimonies like these inspire me to keep going when I get tired and am tempted to quit. I love knowing that God is moving through my music and writing. There's nothing I want more than to do the work the Lord has set before me and help minister to His people. But I face a constant temptation to take an unhealthy pride in what I do to the point of finding my identity in it.

It can be so subtle sometimes, this temptation of pride, especially when we're doing something good. Outwardly, what we're doing may look wonderful, even as we work hard for God's kingdom. But what is going on internally? Are we finding our worth and value in what we do? Are we trying to do it from our own strength, denying that God is the One who ultimately should get the glory? Do we allow compliments and accolades to puff us up? Here's the scariest question I have to ask: *Am I keeping bits of God's glory for myself?*

I'll never forget something I heard Brooke Ligertwood share in a short video about giving God all the glory. She talked about how to receive praise from people. First, don't reject it out of false humility. Instead receive it like they are giving you a flower. Tuck that flower away, and at the end of the day, take all your flowers and give them to God. We should never receive praise from people and keep it for ourselves. Brooke said, "We were made to give glory, never to take it."[1] All the praise should flow back to God. His strength and grace flow into us and give us the ability to accomplish everything we do. Praise for any of what we do should likewise flow back to the Source. It is a dangerous game to keep any of God's glory for ourselves. Like Brooke said, it will poison us on the inside.

These wise words have been a huge help to me in my life and my music career. I am very intentional to gather the flowers of praise I am given and to hand God a beautiful bouquet each day. I can't say I do it perfectly, but I try. God is the originator of my career and the sustainer of it. He should get all the glory from it. I know from experience the peace and joy it brings my heart to give God the glory. I also know the dangers of hanging on to it and letting those words go to my head. It leads to pride, and that is a path I want to avoid at all costs.

TRICKY PRIDE

There are many definitions for *pride* in the dictionary. For the sake of clarity, let me follow the advice of my high school teachers and define my terms. When I use the word *pride*, I am referring to self-centeredness, a focus on yourself that is unhealthy, and thinking more of yourself than you ought. I am referring to wanting and needing praise to make you feel worthy. The Bible likens pride to a "haughty spirit" and makes it clear that pride and a haughty spirit will lead to your downfall (Proverbs 16:18). When we should be keeping our eyes on Jesus and giving Him all the glory, a prideful heart is instead focused on itself and is holding on to bits of the praise and glory meant for the Lord.

But pride is tricky and often masquerades under false names. Even if we act like we're humble and don't want any praise, sometimes our hearts are still feeding on it. In Christian circles, it can appear as good deeds and service to others, but internally, self-righteousness is lurking around. No one else can see what's going on in the deepest places of our souls except for us and God. And even then, sometimes we fool ourselves. That's why we need constant interaction with the Holy Spirit, because only God truly knows the full motives of our hearts. Proverbs 16:2 puts it this way: "All a person's ways seem pure to them, but motives are weighed by the LORD."

The Bible is pretty clear that good deeds alone aren't worth much. Many will say to Jesus that they did so many things in His name, but He will send them away because He never knew them (Matthew 7:21–23). Anything we do that is not grounded in our faith in God does not please Him (Hebrews 11:6). And no matter what we do, if it's not done in love, it's nothing (1 Corinthians 13:1–8). These verses show me three key foundations by which to test my good works:

1. **RELATIONSHIP WITH GOD:** *Is my action flowing out of my relationship with God? Knowing God and being known by God are beyond essential. We don't get to heaven without a real relationship with Jesus. Everything else should flow from this.*
2. **FAITH IN GOD:** *Is my action flowing out of my trust in who God is and what He can do?* Knowing who God is and trusting Him with everything is how we make it through each day. We should not be trusting in ourselves or our own good works but in the completed work of Jesus Christ and in the character of God. Anything we do outside of faith does not please God.
3. **LOVE FOR GOD AND OTHERS:** *Is my action motivated by love?* We can serve at the highest level and be called the greatest Christian in the world, but if we do not have love, we are nothing. Think of this: Jesus summed up the entire Law of God from the Old Testament in two directives for life, both about love.

One of the greatest, if not the greatest, tests to our motivations can be found by comparing them to God's most important instructions for us from Matthew 22:37–40, which says, "'You shall love the Lord

YOUR GOD WITH ALL YOUR HEART, AND WITH ALL YOUR SOUL, AND WITH ALL YOUR MIND.' This is the great and foremost commandment. The second is like it, 'YOU SHALL LOVE YOUR NEIGHBOR AS YOURSELF.' On these two commandments depend the whole Law and the Prophets" (NASB1995).

You might think that pride is always easy to detect, but at times it can disguise itself as any number of personality quirks. Shy people might appear humble but be surprisingly prideful. What seems to be a quiet shyness may be fear of what others think of them and a goal to self-protect. I have a friend who thought her shyness was innocent until God lovingly showed her that it was rooted in pride; she was only thinking about her image and her own comfort. When she started focusing on making others comfortable rather than herself, not only was she able to engage with people better, but her social anxiety diminished as well.

Does it stand to reason, then, that outgoing people are humble? Perhaps. It really depends on the motivation. They might truly be thinking of others first, or they might be trying very hard to please people or get attention for themselves. Similarly, take-charge, type-A personalities might be serving others with their leadership abilities, or they might be operating out of the belief that they are always right, thus things should be done their way. They are unteachable, thinking too highly of themselves. Again, that would be a form of pride because it is all about the self.

I'm not trying to criticize certain personalities here because all personalities have beautiful traits as well as potential inroads for wrong motives or sin. What I'm trying to do is demonstrate the *trickiness* of pride. God gave us so many amazing types of personalities to be celebrated and enjoyed. The key is not to allow the Enemy to sneak in under the guise of "personality quirks." Each and every one of us must open our hearts to the Holy Spirit so He can show us where pockets of pride are hiding, all the while pretending to be something good. Then the best and truest version of our God-given personalities can shine forth.

DANGEROUS TERRITORY

Keeping God's glory for ourselves is a dangerous descent for the Enemy. It can ultimately lead to rebellion against God. I'm all for being a rebel *for* Christ and against the world's system, hence the name and theme of this book. But I shudder at the thought of being a rebel *against* God.

We know for a fact that this is enemy territory. Satan chose pride, rebelled against God, and was thrown out of heaven. Did you know that he was once a beautiful angel who likely led worship in heaven? However, he said in his heart that he would ascend to heaven and be like God, and it led to rebellion and death. He wanted the glory. Satan and the angels who followed him were cast out of heaven forever (Isaiah 14:12; Ezekiel 28:16; Revelation 12:7–9).

Pride is the devil's territory, so it is no wonder that our world is full of it. We are encouraged to take pride in ourselves and to focus on ourselves above all else, even at the expense of others. We are bombarded with temptations to find our identity in what we do, how we look, etc. One peek online and you see it. Social media is full of self-focus and self-promotion. It can easily become a false display centered on gaining likes and followers, all the while keeping people focused only on themselves. We must tread very carefully through these murky waters. I'm not saying social media is all bad because I know it can also be used in truly beneficial ways. I use it myself! What I am saying is to be on guard because it can be a slippery slope into pride.

While the world promotes pride and self-centeredness in a myriad of ways, a Jesus rebel must stand in direct opposition to this mindset. And we do that by following the example that Jesus Himself set for us:

> Have this attitude in yourselves which was also in Christ Jesus, who, although He existed in the form of God, did not regard equality with God a thing to be grasped, but emptied Himself, taking the form of a bond-servant, and being made in the likeness of men. Being found in appearance as a man, He humbled Himself by becoming obedient to the point of death, even death on a cross. (Philippians 2:5–8 NASB1995)

Jesus walked in authority and strength—not pride. There is an enormous difference between these. The wise rebel won't mistake one for the other. Even though Jesus, as the Son of God, had more of a right than any of us ever will, He did not try to grasp equality with God while here on earth. He emptied Himself. He humbled Himself. This was a choice. He chose to live life on earth as a human. He demonstrated for us how to live a Spirit-led life, fully dependent on the Father. He only did what He saw the Father doing and only said what the Father told Him to say. Jesus chose to humble Himself and lay down His life for us, out of His great and perfect love. We are called to follow in His footsteps. We, too, must lay ourselves down and choose humility and a life of love, empowered by the Holy Spirit. When you empty yourself of pride and self-focus, there is room for God to fill you with His power and love. As Matthew 23:12 says, "Whoever exalts himself will be humbled, and whoever humbles himself will be exalted" (ESV).

HUMILITY

On the flip side of pride, we are called to humble ourselves, which means not focusing on ourselves too much and not trying to get glory. Andrew Murray put it this way: "Humility is nothing but the disappearance of self in the vision that God is all."[2] Our goal is not just to avoid thinking too much of ourselves but to set our minds on God, on things above. It's not just to avoid hoarding praise and glory; it's to give God all the praise and glory because only He is worthy. A truly humble person knows that everything she has comes from God. Every talent, strength, ability, skill, and heartbeat is a gift from the almighty Creator. We can take credit for none of it. Instead, we give God all the glory and let His life flow through us to others.

Having a humble heart does not mean you are weak,

timid, or scared. A humble heart is an honest heart. It speaks truth, even in hard situations. When you walk in humility, you don't prioritize your own comfort because you aren't focused on yourself. Instead, you focus on God, who is truth, and on sharing His love with the world. You will have confidence and boldness to speak up and speak out, not because of your strength but because God gives you that boldness. A truly humble person walks in great power—God's power—and knows that everything he has comes straight from God.

Humility also doesn't mean you should bury your gifts and pretend that you're no good. That is false humility. What an insult to the Creator to say that what He made is bad or worthless! True humility brings confidence, not in yourself but in what God is and does through you. If He made you to be an artist, be the best artist you can be *to the glory of God*. If He made you extremely athletic, don't pretend you aren't. But work hard toward excellence so that wherever it takes you, you can give God all the glory! This is true in any area of your life. God gave you a special purpose and unique giftings. He does not want you to be scared or to pretend you have nothing to offer. He wants you to know that it all came from Him and to let your light shine brightly so that people will glorify God when they see it.

My mama and daddy modeled this for Jacob, my sister, Elizabeth, and me while we were growing up. Even though they would encourage and build us up in private, they never bragged on us in public. They didn't feel that bragging on themselves or their children was in obedience to God's Word and knew it would lead to false pride. They taught us to work hard for the glory of God. When people complimented them, I heard them turn it back to God—not fake humility but rather true dependence. Time after time, I saw their consistency in this, and it was deeply ingrained in me. They still set the example for me and help keep me grounded. I continually strive to remember the lessons they modeled for us. I saw them sit in a place of humility and draw their children to it. One of the best ways my parents did this was by constantly giving God praise. A common phrase out of my mama's mouth is, "Oh, thank You, Jesus!" It flows out as naturally as breathing. And she means it.

My family learned the hard way that we depend on God for everything. When we lost Jacob, the only way we were able to survive the pain and heal was through our utter dependence on God. Walking through that deep valley with Jesus has changed us forever. Our life and breath come from Him, and to Him belongs all the praise. On this side of tragedy, our worship is deeper, our humility more genuine, our reliance on God more solid. And it's all because of Him. A humble heart is a heart totally dependent on God and walking in the fullness of life that He alone can give.

WALKING IT OUT

At this point, you might be thinking, *This is all well and good, but what now? What is my next step toward a humble heart?* I can share with you what I've learned from the Word, from experience, and from wise people around me.

It begins with asking God to search your heart and giving Him permission to show you where there are pockets of pride. Here is a good prayer to pray, straight from Scripture: "Search me, O God, and know my heart; try me and know my anxious thoughts; and see if there be any hurtful way in me, and lead me in the everlasting way" (Psalm 139:23–24 NASB1995).

God will lovingly show you the truth of what is in your heart (this is called *conviction*). It might sound scary, but it actually feels like love. Once He does, it's now your job to agree with Him, to confess it, and to repent (change your thinking to match His truth). It might look a little something like this (this can be prayed for any sinful area God shows you, not just pride):

> *Father God, thank You for showing me these hidden motives [or fill in with what He shows you]. I agree with You that I have been trying to hold on to glory; I've been so focused on myself in this. I admit my sin, and I am so sorry. I decide right now to change my thinking and to see this for what it really is. I reject the lies of the Enemy here and break my ties to pride. Please come in, Holy Spirit, to heal my heart and mind and align them with Yours. Thank You for Your forgiveness. I receive it by faith. And I choose to walk in the humble example of my Savior Jesus this day and forever. Amen.*

These aren't magic words—the attitude of your heart is what matters. Be honest and real with God. This isn't one and done either. As you continue to ask God to search your heart, you will continually have opportunities to choose truth and humility. Humble repentance is a lifestyle, as we strive each day to look more like Jesus and less like the world.

Here's one final reminder: No matter where you are in life or what you do, do it all for the glory of God.

Make it your goal that when people look at you, they see a reflection of Jesus and are drawn to Him (not to you). Rebel with all your might against pride and the world's system of self. Continually bring your heart to God and His Word so He can show you the way. In the words of Jesus, "Your light must shine before people in such a way that they may see your good works, and *glorify your Father* who is in heaven" (Matthew 5:16 NASB).

TURNING OUR HEARTS TO JESUS

Dear Jesus,

You are the perfect example of a humble servant. I want to be more like You. I want to know You better and to walk like You walked. Please show me the way. Lead me in the humble way. I will follow You. I pray the words of the apostle Paul: "I have been crucified with Christ; and it is no longer I who live, but Christ who lives in me; and the life which I now live in the flesh I live by faith in the Son of God, who loved me and gave Himself up for me" (Galatians 2:20 NASB).

Amen.

CHAPTER 7

WEAPONS AND WARFARE

We are at war. These powerful words have been uttered across the history of our world too many times to count. Our nation has seen it happen time and again, always with enormous consequences. In my lifetime, there has been war, but not a dramatic beginning like what marked the start of World War II or the days following 9/11. Isn't there so much gravity to the phrase "We are at war"? When these words are spoken in moments like I just mentioned, everyone knows that our lives and our world are about to change forever. I wasn't yet born in 2001, but I have friends who watched the Twin Towers fall. They knew they were seeing history change in that moment. As the reality of what was happening settled on them, they looked at each other and somberly acknowledged, "We are at war."

Do you realize that you are in the midst of a war too, my friend? Satan has been waging war against God and God's people since he was kicked out of heaven. He chose the path of rebelling against God and is trying his hardest to hurt God by hurting the ones He loves. Satan is a thief who wants to steal, kill, and destroy (John 10:10). He is headed for hell and, in a twisted desire for revenge, wants to take as many of God's children with him as he can. He wants to steal, kill, and destroy what God cherishes, and that is you. It's like my mama always says: "The devil hates you with perfect hatred."

But you don't need to be afraid! Jesus has already defeated Satan—He conquered Satan when He died on the cross and was raised from the dead. Jesus has victory over Satan, sin, and death. "Therefore, since the children share in flesh and blood, He Himself likewise also partook of the same, that through death He might render powerless him who had the power of death, that is, the devil, and might free those who through fear of death were subject to slavery all their lives" (Hebrews 2:14–15 NASB1995).

Then isn't the war over, Anne? you may ask. Well, yes and no. Jesus already has victory through His finished work and resurrection, and He invites us into it. He took back what humans gave away in the garden of Eden. The Bible also tells us that at the end of time, there will be a great war, and Satan will be thrown into the lake of fire forever. Then it will be over for good. But here we are, in the in-between. We are still on this earth, fighting the fight of faith. And it is a battle for our souls. We still have an enemy and must choose every single day whether we are following Jesus or not. We must walk out our faith and persevere until the end. And our Enemy is roaming this earth looking for the ones he can devour (1 Peter 5:8). My questions to you are: Do you know that you are in a war? And are you prepared for it?

The amazing news about this war is that we know how it ends—total victory over the Enemy and eternal reward for God's people. Incredible! On earth, nations enter into war without knowing how it will end. They may have plans, strategies, and probabilities . . . but they don't *know* until it is over. But in this war, we know *now*. God wins. We win. Satan loses.

And yet . . . we still have to fight the good fight while we run our race here on earth. The Enemy will not stop trying to destroy us until we cross the finish line (1 Timothy 6:12). But never forget that we are fighting *from* a place of victory, not for it. Jesus already did that.

BE AWARE

We never want to focus on Satan too much—because he loves attention. And because our focus should be on the Lord instead. It is important, however, to be aware of the attacks of the Enemy. We don't want to be blindsided or to naively fall into one of his traps. So let's look at some of the ways the Enemy attacks.

I believe that the Enemy studies us and knows our areas of weakness. Therefore, he attacks individual people in different ways—but always with similar patterns. Here are some important characteristics that God has shown us about our Enemy through His Word:

- Satan masquerades as an angel of light. He tries to deceive us, trick us, and appear to be something good. "No wonder, for even Satan disguises himself as an angel of light." (2 Corinthians 11:14 NASB)
- Satan is a thief who wants to steal, kill, and destroy. "The thief comes only to steal and kill and destroy." (John 10:10 NASB)
- He is the father of lies. He will always try to get you to believe lies about God and about yourself. "You are of your father the devil, and you want to do the desires of your father. He was a murderer

from the beginning, and does not stand in the truth because there is no truth in him. Whenever he speaks a lie, he speaks his own nature, because he is a liar and the father of lies." (John 8:44 NASB)

- He fell because of pride, and he tries to trick us into it too. (Isaiah 14; Ezekiel 28)

I have seen these kinds of attacks play out in my own life, especially in the area of lying. Our Enemy tries to get us to believe his lies and to hold us captive through them. Whenever I'm about to step onstage, I often get hit with attacks like this from the Enemy. It happens consistently, but it is usually more intense when the audience is larger or is less likely to know Jesus. Negative thoughts try to fill my mind, such as: *You aren't enough. They're making fun of you. You aren't pretty enough. You're going to fail. No one is impressed with you.* The list goes on.

I know now that these are lies from the Enemy—because he doesn't want me to share the good news of Jesus. With his deceitful words, he's trying to destroy my testimony by holding me captive to fear and shame. He wants to get me nervous and too afraid to tell people about my Jesus.

Do you know what defeats lies? The truth. I've

already shared some stories with you about how God uses my family and friends to speak truth to me in those moments. And that truth always prevails. As John 8:32 says, "You will know the truth, and the truth will make you free" (NASB1995). Satan's lies enslave us and keep us captive. But God's truth sets us free. Every time.

In the summer of 2025, I was headed into the studio to record the title track for my new album, *Stars*. As I approached the microphone, I felt my voice tighten up to the point that I could not sing. What in the world was this? I tried again, with the same result. It felt like my vocal cords were tensed up so tightly that they didn't work. By this point in my life, I am more aware of the Enemy's attacks, and I knew that's what was happening. He wanted to stop this album and to steal what God is going to do through it.

I have also experienced the temptation to give in to pride instead of giving God the glory. That is a sneaky and dangerous trap, like we saw in the last chapter. At other times, I have experienced the Enemy trying to masquerade his plans in good-sounding words and ideas while all along it's a plan to steal my identity and God-given purpose. *Just change yourself and compromise a little here and a little there so more people will listen to you.* But these lies are always in direct opposition to who

God made me to be and the unique identity He gave me. They're a trap.

When I was in high school, my class read *The Screwtape Letters* by C. S. Lewis. This book is an imaginative way to look at the subtle plans the Enemy might be laying for us. It's a fascinating book that really opened my eyes to areas in my life where I was giving ground to the Enemy. One of those areas was how I viewed my parents. I held prideful and rebellious attitudes in my heart toward them based on lies I was believing about them. I felt led to repent (think new thoughts) about what I was doing. I decided to stop believing the Enemy's lies and instead humble myself to my parents and get in line with God's truth about who they are and how I am to honor them.

What about you? Are you aware of the ways the Enemy is trying to steal, kill, and destroy you? Do you recognize his lies? Can you spot the traps he's laying for you?

The best thing to do, even if you think you already know the answer, is to ask God. Come humbly to Him and ask Him to show you the lies you're believing about Him and about yourself. Have a pen and paper ready. Write down what you hear without analyzing it first. You may be surprised by what He shows you. Pray through whatever it is. Surrender it to God. Then I suggest that you destroy that paper because it is full of lies. And get ready to receive His truth. It isn't enough just to expose the lies of the Enemy. We must replace them with truth from God. So get a new piece of paper. You know what to do. Ask and listen. Write down what you hear. Whatever the situation or the lie you need to replace, God will have the answer. Listen and receive. Test it against the Word of God. The truth will set you free.

WORSHIP IS A WEAPON

Let's revisit that moment in the recording studio when my vocal cords tightened up and I couldn't sing. I was aware of the Enemy's attack, and that led me to take action. I paused the session and stepped out to have a private moment. First, I texted Erica to tell her what was going on and to ask her to please pray for me right that moment. Next I put on worship music and went straight to God in prayer. He is always the answer—His name, His blood, His finished work, His power. After worshipping and praying for a little while, I returned to the studio and was not only able to sing but to finish the album that day!

In the middle of battle, one of the most powerful weapons a believing rebel has against the forces of evil is worship. Worship puts our focus back on the Lord and declares the truth of who He is. We thank Him in advance—right in the middle of the turmoil—for His victory. We don't have to know the details of exactly how He'll answer us. We can come to Him in faith, knowing that He never fails and is greater than any attack of the Enemy and that we can worship Him right then and there. The Enemy wants our attention to be on *anything* other than God because he knows God is where the power is. Whether we get focused on ourselves, on others, or on the attack against us, the devil just wants us worried and distracted. But we can refuse to give in. We can *rebel* against him and worship God in the middle of the battle.

You can see examples of this in the Bible too. In Judges 6 and 7, when God called Gideon to lead a tiny army of Israelites against a huge horde of Midianites, the first thing God commanded Gideon to do was destroy the altar to a fake god and build an altar to the true God instead. Yes, they were facing a huge army and potential destruction, but first things first—worship the Lord your God. Put Him first.

Later, the nation of Judah was invaded by a great

multitude of warriors from other countries (2 Chronicles 20). They turned to the Lord in prayer, led by their king, Jehoshaphat. He prayed an honest prayer to God and ended with these words: "O our God, will You not judge them? For we are powerless before this great multitude who are coming against us; nor do we know what to do, but our eyes are on You" (v. 12 NASB1995). They were scared and powerless. They had no idea what to do. They admitted all of this to God and turned their eyes to Him only. And His battle plan for them was essentially this: *Don't be afraid. I will fight this battle. You are to send out worshippers as the first ones against the enemy* (vv. 15–17). When the people obeyed God's instructions and sent the worshippers into battle first (a strategy that makes no logical sense to the human brain), He sent an ambush against the enemy and caused them to literally destroy themselves.

Here is what stands out to me from these examples. No matter how the odds may seem stacked against us, we are on the side of the God of the universe, who never fails and never loses. He can solve any problem and has strategies for victory that are far beyond what our minds can come up with. The battle ultimately belongs to Him, not us. Our job is to turn our eyes to God, pray honest prayers (fully admitting our fears and failures, like Gideon and Jehoshaphat did), and worship Him through it all. Our job is also to obey. Whatever strategy God gives us as we listen in prayer, we must obey. We might look crazy to the world; we might look like rebels to common sense even. But think about it—what makes more sense in the midst of a battle than to follow the One who created the entire universe and is incapable of losing?

Whatever battle you're in right now, I encourage you to take some time with God. Step outside the studio, so to speak. Worship Him, tell Him the truth of how you feel and what you're afraid of, ask for His help, and listen for His battle plan. Call on other believers to stand with you and pray for you. Then rest in His goodness, because just as He said to the people of Judah, He says to you, "Do not fear or be dismayed because of this great multitude, for the battle is not yours but God's" (2 Chronicles 20:15 NASB1995).

WISE ADVICE

We can learn so much by listening to the wise advice of those who are further down the road than we are. That is why I have people in my life like my parents, Erica,

Pastor Cameron, and others. I call on them when I need prayer and encouragement. They give me advice on how to face attacks from the Evil One.

My mama has instilled in me from a young age how powerful worship is. When I was a little girl, she told me how to handle a bad dream. She would say, "Sweetheart, if you wake up from a bad dream, I want you to start singing 'Jesus Loves Me,' and you'll drift back to sleep in no time." And she was right. I even started playing worship music in my room 24-7, which gave me the best sleep of my life! To this day, if I am tormented by a nightmare and wake up in fear, I will ask Jesus to help me. Then I'll start singing a worship song. It always brings me peace so I can go right back to sleep.

God gave me another precious mentor when I was twelve years old named Pastor Tim. He was there supporting our family through the loss of Jacob and my entrance into the music industry. He used to meet me out on tour just so he could pray over me and my band. He instilled a deep love of Jesus in me and an understanding of how to listen to God's voice. And I began following his pattern for prayer. He always started his prayers this way: "I plead the blood of Jesus and declare that only the Holy Spirit may come close and prosper." This brought a level of focus to my prayers that made them feel more powerful. And it declared that the Enemy was not allowed to come near when I was talking with and listening to God.

Pastor Tim went home to Jesus in spring 2025, before any of us were ready for him to leave. It was so hard to say goodbye. But I know that since the Father took him home, Pastor Tim had finished his race. He fought the good fight. And he showed so many people how to come humbly to the feet of Jesus and hear His voice. At his memorial service, everyone received a little red bracelet that said, "I plead the blood of Jesus." Why was this statement so powerful that it marked his entire ministry? Because there is power in the blood of Jesus. It washes us white as snow and protects us from the Evil One.

In the book of Revelation, John described war in heaven and the defeat of Satan. He said this about how believers overcame the Enemy's accusations: "They overcame him because of the blood of the Lamb and the word of their testimony, and they did not love their life even when faced with death" (12:11 NASB1995). May we be covered in the blood of Jesus, the Lamb of God. May we share the truth of what He has done for us with others and be willing to lay our lives down for Him, day in and day out. There is so much power there.

John Eldredge's books and ministry have greatly impacted my life. So of course I want to tell you about how! The advice and wisdom he shares in his book *Walking with God* taught me a great deal about the spiritual battle we're fighting and the kinds of prayers that are effective in that battle.[1] Prayer is extremely powerful, especially when we listen to God in prayer and understand His heart for us and for others. Then we pray along with His will instead of just complaining or telling Him what we want. Prayer brings us back into connection with God and aligns our thinking with His truth.

I have found in my own walk that worship and prayer are the two practices I draw on most when I sense an attack from the Enemy. Yes, we want to be aware of the Enemy's tactics, but more than anything, we want to be focused on the Lord. I turn to God, set my heart on Him, and trust Him with the outcome. Prayer and worship can help you do just that.

STAND FIRM

Sometimes, when I face the lying attacks of the Enemy, I know that the best strategy I have is to resist and stand firm. For me, this means staying true to what I know the Lord has called me to do. I may feel shaky, but I walk out onstage anyway. I may face ridicule, but I stay true to my message of Jesus' love and salvation. I continue to obey God and persevere in what He has done rather than give in to believing the lies of the Evil One.

In the book of James, we find a very powerful verse about spiritual warfare. Right in the middle of talking about the importance of humility, James gave us this profound truth: "Submit therefore to God. Resist the devil and he will flee from you" (4:7 NASB1995). We humble ourselves before God and submit to all His ways. And we *resist* the devil. We refuse to believe his lies. We do not obey what he wants or the systems of this world. We plant ourselves firmly in the Lord. This is the heart of a Jesus rebel. And as we already discussed, taking a stand cannot be done in our own strength. So when the Lord calls you to resist the lies of the Enemy or the systems of this world, it is vital to know that *He* is the one who gives you the strength and authority to remain steadfast. Is there an area in your life where God is calling you to stand firm? Take a moment to journal about that so you can return to it each day for encouragement.

We see this advice repeated in a letter the apostle Paul wrote to the church in Ephesus:

> Finally, be strong in the Lord and in the strength of His might. Put on the full armor of God, so that you will be able to stand firm against the schemes of the devil. For our struggle is not against flesh and blood, but against the rulers, against the powers, against the world forces of this darkness, against the spiritual forces of wickedness in the heavenly places. Therefore, take up the full armor of God, so that you will be able to resist in the evil day, and having done everything, to stand firm. (Ephesians 6:10–13 NASB1995)

You can hold out against the devil's lies and schemes only in the Lord's strength and in the armor He gives us. It is only through the finished work of Jesus Christ that we have any victory whatsoever. I encourage you to put on the armor of God each day in your prayer time: the belt of truth, the breastplate of righteousness, the shoes of the gospel of peace, the shield of faith, the helmet of salvation, and the sword of the Spirit, which is the Word of God (Ephesians 6:14–18). Each of these pieces of the armor is provided by God alone. He is the truth and He gives us His righteousness. We tell the good news (the gospel) of the salvation He freely offers us. Faith is a gift from God. And we take up our one offensive weapon: the sword of the Spirit, which is the Word of God.

THE WORD OF GOD

The Word of God (also called Scripture, or the Bible) is our weapon in the spiritual war for our souls. It is the truth we stand firmly on and hold tightly to. We replace the lies of the Evil One with the truth of God, revealed in His Word. In order to use the sword of the Spirit, which is the Word of God, we must know and study it. Spend time reading God's Word each day to arm yourself for the daily battle.

If spending time in God's Word is new for you, or if you'd like some fresh ideas on how to spend that time, I'd love to give you a glimpse into what I do when I open the Bible. I have done various Bible studies written by believers I admire, and those can be immensely helpful. Currently, however, I'm not following a particular study. I choose a book of the Bible to study and work my way through it slowly. Each day, I plead the blood of Jesus over my time with Him and ask God to reveal to me all He wants to show me through His Word. It sometimes helps to read aloud because it slows me down and causes me to focus. Sometimes I find myself praying a portion of Scripture aloud to God, letting His Word guide my requests and form my desires. And I always keep my journal with me to write down what God is highlighting, questions I have, or prayers I'm offering up to Him. Keep in mind that the Word of God is our daily bread. You may not always *feel* like you've had a transformative time, but rest assured that His Word is nourishing you and strengthening you, even when you aren't aware of it. You are arming yourself for life's battle with the sword of the Spirit, which is the Word of God (Ephesians 6:17).

Jesus Himself used scriptures as His weapon against the devil when facing a great temptation from Satan. Jesus had just finished a forty-day fast in the wilderness when Satan came to Him and tried to get Him to fall. The first temptation focused on Jesus' physical state of hunger and His identity: "If you are the Son of God, tell these stones to become bread." But Jesus responded with truth from the Scriptures: "It is written: 'Man shall not live on bread alone, but on every word that comes from the mouth of God'" (Matthew 4:3–4).

Then Satan took Jesus to the pinnacle of the temple and tempted Him to prove God's love for Him, a spiritual test. *Throw Yourself down*, Satan said, *because the Scriptures say God will save you with His angels*. This paraphrase of verses 5–6 shows that Satan will also try to use the words of God against us. Yes, he does know what they say. That's why it is so vital to have a relationship with the Author of the Bible—so that His Holy

Spirit can help you rightly discern His truth and not be tricked by the Evil One. Again, Jesus used the Word of God as His weapon, saying, "It is also written: 'Do not put the Lord your God to the test'" (v. 7).

Finally, Satan brought the biggest temptation of all: a perverted shortcut to the end goal and the deep desire of Jesus' heart. Jesus came to rescue and redeem all humankind. Satan offered Him all the kingdoms of the world if Jesus would just bow down and worship Satan. But Jesus was not fooled. He knew there was no easy way out to get His reward. What Satan offered was enslavement and death. Jesus knew what was right and true, and He ended it then and there: "Away from me, Satan! For it is written: 'Worship the Lord your God, and serve him only'" (v. 10).

If the Word of God is what Jesus used against the temptations of the Evil One, that is exactly what we should do too. Stand firm on the Word of God.

WHAT A WONDERFUL NAME

No matter what battle or temptation you face, what lies you hear, or what fear you feel, there is one that you can always call on for help—the wonderful, powerful name of Jesus.

In the book of Luke, we read about Jesus sending out seventy of His followers to go into other cities and preach about the kingdom of God. When they came back to Jesus, they were filled with joy at what they had experienced. They said, "Lord, even the demons are subject to us in Your name" (10:17 NASB1995). They had watched Jesus perform miracles and cast out demons, but now they had experienced the same thing through the name and authority of Jesus. They discovered the power of the name of Jesus Christ, our Savior!

Have you experienced the power of the name of Jesus? Sometimes, when I am desperate or unable to pray long prayers, I simply breathe a one-word prayer, "Jesus!" He already knows what is in my heart and what I need. I cry out to Him. All my prayers and declarations are made in the mighty name of Jesus because I believe what the Bible says about His beautiful name.

> For this reason also, God highly exalted Him, and bestowed on Him the name which is above every name, so that at the name of Jesus EVERY KNEE WILL BOW, of those who are in heaven and on earth and under the earth, and that every tongue will confess that Jesus Christ is Lord, to the glory of God the Father. (Philippians 2:9–11 NASB1995)

TURNING OUR HEARTS TO JESUS

Would you pray this one out loud, friends?

I plead the blood of Jesus and declare that only the Holy Spirit may come close and prosper. I come in the mighty name of Jesus, my Savior. Lord God, I ask You to reveal Your truth to me in new ways. Help me to rightly discern what is of You and what is not. Help me to resist the devil. Expose the lies I have believed and replace them with Your truth. Rebuke the Enemy on my behalf, Lord God. Lead me not into temptation, but deliver me from evil. You are the eternal Victor, the Champion of my life, the Savior of the world. I trust You. I love You. I worship You. May Your will be done in my life above all else. Fill me afresh with Your Holy Spirit, and lead me in the way everlasting.
Amen.

CHAPTER 8

THE RESTFUL HEART OF A REBEL

I was chatting with my mom recently about the busyness of life for families in America right now. With people running from one activity to the next and working hard to check off their to-do lists, there is so little time for family connection and rest. When I ask friends how their summer was, the answer is usually, "It's been super busy!" And almost everyone I know is "in a busy season of life" right now. But does that season ever end? We are all hustling through life, and we are all exhausted. Is this what we were meant for? My mom summed it up pretty well when she said, "It's like a cruel joke has been played on us."

The more I think about it, the more I realize that she is exactly right. Satan, the Enemy of our souls, *has* played a cruel joke on us. He lured us in with promises of productivity and purpose. But the not-so-funny punch line is a life filled with worry, distraction, and busyness leading to burnout and disconnection from God. Our souls cannot keep up with the pace of this driven culture. And the devil knows it. A quote often attributed to Corrie ten Boom puts it this way: "If the devil can't make you sin, he'll make you busy."

What is a rebel's response to this hectic, soul-crushing culture of busyness and hurried activity? It's rest, quiet, and time alone with God. I love what John Mark Comer says in his book *The Ruthless Elimination of Hurry*: "Here's my point: the solution to an overbusy life is *not* more time. It's to slow down and simplify our lives around what really matters."[1] I can tell you from personal experience that this does not come easily. Slowing down is so countercultural that we truly need to be rebels against the drive to fill our days with constant activity and our minds with worried thoughts (not to mention that an overbusy life will fill our bodies with stress, which can lead to all kinds of sickness).

Like we talked about in the previous chapter, you are in a battle for your soul. And the Enemy will do everything he can to destroy you. One of his cleverest and most destructive tactics is to get you to fill your life so full of seemingly good things that you are worn down, stressed out, disconnected from yourself, disconnected from your loved ones, and—scariest of all—disconnected from God. I know because I've been there.

Take a moment to do a quick inventory. How does your body feel in this moment? What muscles are tensed? Is your jaw clenched? Is your stomach tight? Are thoughts racing through your mind? Are you fighting distraction even now? Take three deep breaths, and relax your mind and body. Maybe close your eyes and just tell Jesus that you love Him and you trust Him. Stay there a moment.

Now, friend, let's talk about rest. We all desperately need it, but rest doesn't just happen. We cannot wait for the perfect moment to present itself in order to rest. We must fight for it. We have to relentlessly pursue rest. It's time to rebel against the busy, distracted life the Enemy wants to keep us ensnared in. As the Bible tells us, "Let us therefore *strive* to enter that rest, so that no one may fall by the same sort of disobedience" (Hebrews 4:11 ESV).

REST IS NOT AN OPTION

I find the word *disobedience* in the scripture above interesting—and rather alarming. Does entering God's rest prevent us from falling away because of disobedience? Is it disobedient not to rest? It actually is!

In the book of Exodus, God tells us about how He delivered His people from slavery in Egypt through a man named Moses. Then God met with Moses on Mount Sinai and gave him the Ten Commandments, which are ten rules for God's people to follow. You've probably heard of them or maybe even know them by heart. They include instructions like not worshipping idols, not murdering, not stealing, etc. But there is also one about rest. Did you know that? Take a look at Exodus 20:8–11:

> Remember the sabbath day, to keep it holy. Six days you shall labor and do all your work, but the seventh day is a sabbath of the LORD your God; in it you shall not do any work, you or your son or your daughter, your male or your female servant or your cattle or your sojourner who stays with you. For in six days the LORD made the heavens and the earth, the sea and all that is in them, and rested on the seventh day; therefore the LORD blessed the sabbath day and made it holy. (NASB1995)

Just as God rested from His work, He commands us to take a rest day after six days of work. The Jewish people take their rest day (or Sabbath) on Saturdays. Most Christians view Sunday as their day of rest. What about you? Do you have a true day of rest? Personally, I intentionally take a day away from work and the world each week, although it isn't always on a Sunday. And sometimes I only get half a day. But no matter how I do it each week, I work hard to make it a priority rather than an afterthought, which means scheduling around it. I put my phone away, resist the urge to look at emails, and spend time doing what restores my soul. It looks different week to week, but that's okay. What matters is that it happens.

Most of us wouldn't *dare* break the "big" commandments, like not murdering and not stealing. But we don't bat an eye at breaking the commandment to keep the Sabbath. Whether we are ignoring it or think it doesn't apply to us, we pass right on by it and stay busy, busy, busy. Our days are filled with activities and tasks that seem good, important, and vital to our success. Whether it is sports, work, volunteering, being productive at home, cleaning, cooking, or one of numerous other time fillers, it all appears to be worthy of our time, to the point that we fill all our days to the max. Then we wonder why we are stressed, anxious, burned out, and depressed. This soul-deep exhaustion happens in large part because we ignore the directions our Creator gave us for how to live. He knows our bodies and our souls better than we do. He knows what kind of rest we need and how often we need it. His direction to us to rest is for our own good! In addition to that, God wants us to give Him one of our most valuable commodities: our time.

Notice that we are told to rest because God rested. After six days of work to create the entire universe, including all that is in the earth, God rested from His work. And we are supposed to do as we see our Father doing, just like Jesus demonstrated for us. Let's revisit that Hebrews passage and back up a few verses to see what God says about Sabbath in the New Testament: "So then, there remains a Sabbath rest for the people of God, for whoever has entered God's rest has also rested from his works as God did from his. Let us therefore strive to enter that rest, so that no one may fall by the same sort of disobedience" (4:9–11 ESV). After all that Jesus has done for us, there remains a rest for the people of God. We are to follow in our Father's footsteps and diligently work to enter His rest. I encourage you not to disobey this command, no matter how tempting it may be. If you do, life will get much harder for you.

LEARNING TO REST

I grew up in a busy household, with a family who all worked extremely hard. Before he passed away, my brother was preparing for law school. My sister runs her own clothing company. My mom has been a teacher, run a business, and started two schools. From engineering to supporting my sister's company and traveling with me, my dad has always put in extremely long workdays. And I am a to-do-list kind of girl. I like to work hard and perform well. Staying busy and working hard comes naturally to us. Rest, however, does not. I have had to learn how to rest—and why it matters so much!

I launched into my music career while still in high school and trying to juggle my schoolwork and home life at the same time. From there, it only got busier and harder as I stepped into touring, songwriting, interviews, recording, and many tasks I never knew were part of a music career. I reached a point that I went seventy-five days straight with no day off.

I let myself become very run-down, and I didn't really know what rest looked like. It was during that time that the Lord began teaching me to rely on His strength instead of my own. He also began to teach me about the importance of a Sabbath rest. God spoke to me through my counselor and the books of John Mark Comer, like the one I mentioned earlier, to guide me down this path. And, yes, He even worked through my hitting rock bottom to grow me into a better understanding and practice of rest. That's how He got my attention and showed me that I could not continue the way I was going. I had to figure out a pattern of rest that worked with my grueling schedule. I was determined to find a weekly Sabbath rest—and also to carve out time each day to be with God.

Weekends sometimes aren't an option for me to take a Sabbath since I have shows on many weekends. And when I'm on tour, my evenings are spent on a bus rather than in the privacy of my home. That means I have to get creative and tenacious about prioritizing times of recuperation. If I don't intentionally pull away for time alone, I will quickly start to get run-down. I can tell that I have neglected my Sabbath when I become physically worn out or sick and when I become mentally overwhelmed with worries and endless to-do lists. At times like this, I usually feel like I'm performing from an empty tank. I'm not giving my best because I've run out of reserve. I know in these moments that I need some extra time with God. What I give to others should come from an overflow of what I receive from God in private. If I'm not getting alone with God to receive from Him, what do I have to give away?

You may have a life schedule that does not make Sabbath rest easy or normal. You might work weekends, play competitive sports, have little ones to take care of 24-7, or have an extremely demanding job. And you just can't seem to find time to rest. But that means you have to *make* the time. Make resting with God a priority in your life, even if it comes on a different day than others' Sabbaths or at odd times. I try to get time alone with God every single day as well as reserve a day of rest within my week. He is my source and supply. When I don't prioritize these times with Him, I become overwhelmed quickly because I'm trying to do it in my own strength.

Your Sabbath rest might not look like everyone else's either. That's okay. Let the Lord lead you into what is the best form of rest for you. And I'm not talking about just pampering yourself, shutting everyone out, or bingeing shows or scrolling on social media. I'm talking about doing the things that restore your soul and give rest to your body. For me, that means quality time with friends and family and having fun. As I mentioned earlier, I intentionally stay off my phone and put work aside for the day (or however many hours I can carve out). I have heard it said that if you do physical labor for your career, you will need to engage your mind on your rest days. And if you have a mentally challenging job, you might need physical activity as part of your Sabbath. This will allow the overworked part of your being to rest and recover.

But above all, your soul needs quality time with God. You need to make space to get alone with God, quiet your soul, and listen to Him. Talk to Him. Learn from Him. Jesus Himself modeled this for us when He lived on earth. We read in Luke 5:15–16 about how, at the height of His ministry and with growing fame, Jesus maintained His time alone with Father God: "The news about Him was spreading even farther, and large crowds were gathering to hear Him and to be healed of their sicknesses. But Jesus Himself would often slip away to the wilderness and pray" (NASB). There was probably never a moment that seemed convenient for Jesus to just disappear and go meet with His Father in the wilderness. His disciples were probably scared and wondering where He was. I imagine that the people who came in large crowds to hear Him and be healed by Him wanted more, more, more. They were desperate for what He offered. But Jesus had His priorities in line and regularly slipped away from all the good He was doing to be alone with Father God and be replenished.

When He came back from time with the Father, Jesus knew what to do and what His next step was. He received strength, instruction, comfort, and knowledge. If Jesus Himself needed time alone with the Father, how much more do we? Like John Mark Comer says, "If you don't set aside time to be alone with God, your relationship will wither on the vine."[2]

EXCHANGING GOOD FOR BEST

Do you find it hard to make time for resting with God because of the many things you need to do? You have responsibilities and demands that you cannot simply ignore, right? People are counting on you. You feel guilty for taking time for yourself. I get that. I struggle with it too. It took me a while to realize that it is important to speak up about what I need. My family and my management team don't know what I need unless I tell them. So when I realize that I am weary and God is calling me to rest, I vocalize that to my team. The same is true for you. Your boss, your family, your spouse, your friends—none of them can know what you need or when it's time for you to get alone with God unless you tell them.

After sharing what you need, you will probably be

faced with many opportunities to say no to good things in order to say yes to the best thing—time with God. I have chosen to say no to show offers or other opportunities that arise because I could sense that the Lord was telling me to rest and get alone with Him. And I couldn't do both. It isn't always easy to say no like this, and it requires a big dose of faith. But *no* is an incredibly important word. A true yes to God will mean saying no to whatever is threatening to take His place in your life.

There is a story in the Bible that I love and deeply identify with. It's about two sisters, Mary and Martha. They were extremely close to Jesus, and He often stayed at their home when traveling nearby. One time when Jesus was there, Martha busied herself with preparations and cooking while Mary sat at Jesus' feet to listen. Martha was doing good work. I imagine she was trying to honor the Lord and make her home and her food a lovely offering to Him. But she had stepped outside worshipful service and into worry, stress, and distraction. I can totally identify. Can you? Finally, she came to Jesus and told Him how she felt.

> Martha was distracted by all the preparations that had to be made. She came to him and asked, "Lord, don't you care that my sister has left me to do the work by

> myself? Tell her to help me!" "Martha, Martha," the Lord answered, "you are worried and upset about many things, but few things are needed—or indeed only one. Mary has chosen what is better, and it will not be taken away from her." (Luke 10:40–42)

I encourage you to put your name in place of Martha's in Jesus' response. What would He tell you to lay down so that you can sit at His feet and listen to His voice? Can you be as honest with Jesus as Martha was? Tell Him exactly what you're stressed and worried about. Be brutally honest. And then listen for what He wants to say to you—for the truth He will speak to you. Lay down what seems so good and important to you. Only one thing is truly necessary. Come to Jesus. Are you weary and burdened? He is inviting you to sit at His feet and find rest for your soul. "Come to me, all you who are weary and burdened, and I will give you rest" (Matthew 11:28).

REST MEANS TRUST

When I say no to great opportunities out of obedience to God, it requires me to trust the outcome to Him. I choose to believe that He will provide other opportunities for me and take care of the ones I said no to. He will provide. If I can't say no when God is asking me to because I'm afraid I'll lose out or will upset people, it means I'm not actually trusting God. If I think I must handle it rather than trusting that He will, that is actually a form of pride. When you think about these responses, they reveal that deep down, we believe it all depends on us.

When you sit down in a chair, do you trust that chair? Are you fully relaxed or are you constantly braced for impact because the chair might fail at any moment? Trusting God means you can relax in His presence and trust Him to hold you up. You can rest knowing that God will provide what you and others need. He will not fail you. Give everything and everyone to Him, trust Him with the outcomes, and rest with God. It is a beautiful act of faith.

Sometimes God will call you to rest in the middle of a battle or an incredibly stressful time. It seems counterintuitive because the world would tell you to fight harder and work faster in those moments. But God's kingdom doesn't follow the patterns of this world. God's kingdom goes against our human logic and follows a greater truth. Resting in the Lord can be an amazing weapon of warfare because you are trusting God completely, obeying His voice, and surrendering the outcome to Him. He will fight for you.

Did you know that you can tell your soul to rest? You can command it, just like David did when he said, "Yes, my soul, find rest in God; my hope comes from him. Truly he is my rock and my salvation; he is my fortress, I will not be shaken" (Psalm 62:5–6). Maybe it's time to turn your heart to Jesus and command your soul—your mind, will, and emotions—to rest. It may seem scary to let go of control of *all the things*, but I promise you can trust Him. Every time I obey His leading to surrender something that seems good in order to get time with God, He always provides something better. He is always the best choice. I encourage you to try it. Be honest with Him, like Martha was, and listen for His invitation to come away. Jesus is the one thing we need.

LISTEN AND OBEY

It is extremely tempting to try to prove ourselves to God and earn His love. We wouldn't say it out loud, but our actions make clear what we believe deep inside. We work so hard *for* God, but how much do we spend time *with* God? We think He only wants our service and sacrifice when He really wants our hearts. Serving God is an overflow of our love relationship with Him. He created us for that kind of relationship. How many of us believe the lie that we must work to be accepted by God? Pause here and let God show you the truth. If you did nothing for God today, would you feel guilty or would you know that His love toward you has not changed one iota?

When we live out of the lie that we have to earn His love, we deny the power of the cross and resurrection. Jesus already did it all for us so that we can be accepted and adopted as beloved children of God. We could never work hard enough or be good enough to even come close to what Jesus already freely offers us because of His great love for us.

What does He ask for in return? Jesus said, "If you love Me, you will keep My commandments" (John 14:15 NASB). We know that includes the Ten Commandments and all His words in the New Testament. In fact, while on earth, Jesus summed up the total of all the law and prophets with these words: "'You shall love the Lord your God with all your heart, with all your soul, and with all your mind.' This is the great and foremost commandment. The second is like it, 'You shall love your neighbor as yourself.' On these two commandments depend the whole Law and the Prophets" (Matthew 22:37–40 NASB1995).

Love the Lord your God. How? By obeying Him. By

putting Him first. By spending time with Him. By making Him the priority in every single aspect of your life.

God tells us to rest and to spend private time with Him. We, as rebels for Jesus, must obey His command no matter how crazy we seem to the world. We know that "to obey is better than sacrifice" (1 Samuel 15:22 NASB1995). The world says to run faster, work harder, stay busy. Instead, we slow down and get alone with God. We put first things first. We stop trying so hard in our own strength and start trusting our Father. We listen and obey. Because of love.

Let's end this chapter by meditating a moment on these words from the book of Isaiah: "This is what the Sovereign LORD, the Holy One of Israel, says: 'In repentance and rest is your salvation, in quietness and trust is your strength'" (30:15).

Come to Jesus, and He will give you rest.

TURNING OUR HEARTS TO JESUS

Precious Lord Jesus,

I am weary and burdened. I am worried and distracted. I'm afraid that You don't care about what I'm carrying. I'm scared that it will all fall apart if

I let go in surrender. [You might need to mention specific areas of your life where this is true for you.] I repent of believing the lies that You will not provide all I need and that I have to carry it myself. I repent of the pride that says it all depends on me. I come to You, Jesus, to receive Your rest. I choose to believe that You will not fail me. Help me trust You so deeply and so fully that I can truly rest in Your presence. I lay down my whole life so that You can live Your life through me and fill me with joy and peace. You promised that You will keep in perfect peace the one whose mind is fixed on You (Isaiah 26:3). So I fix my mind and heart on You and sit at Your feet to listen. You are the One thing I desperately need. Thank You for loving me. I love You.

Now linger in His presence and let His love wash over you.

CHAPTER 9

RELENTLESS PURSUIT

What you behold, you become.

This commonly shared belief has proven true not only in my own life but also throughout the ages. What we put before our eyes and in our minds, we will become like. The people you surround yourself with will influence who you become. What you focus your time, money, and energy on will be not only the goal of your life but also your master. With this in mind, I ask you: What are you beholding? What do you fix your heart and mind on each day? What matters most to you?

The world encourages us to chase after the things that are not eternal—fame, beauty, success, influence, wealth, etc. But Jesus tells us to walk the other way, to "seek first the kingdom of God and his righteousness, and all these things will be added to you" (Matthew 6:33 ESV). If you read the full context of that verse, Jesus isn't saying we will automatically get wealth, fame, and glory. He is saying not to worry about even the most basic things like clothing or food because, when we put God first, He will provide everything we need. And we can trust Him to know exactly what we need.

THE ONE THING THAT MATTERS

Do you remember from our previous chapter what Jesus said to Martha when she was upset that Mary wasn't helping her with preparations for their guests? He told her that only "one thing" is necessary (Luke 10:42). Martha had many distractions, worries, and a strong desire to please, but just *one thing* really mattered: sitting at the feet of Jesus to listen and learn. In other words, beholding Jesus.

In the Gospel of Mark, there is the story of a man who ran up to Jesus and asked what he needed to do to inherit eternal life. Jesus mentioned to him the commandments about how to treat his fellow man, which the man said he had kept since he was a child. Then

Jesus went to the heart level. He said, "*One thing* you lack: go and sell all you possess and give to the poor, and you will have treasure in heaven; and come, follow Me" (Mark 10:21 NASB).

Instead of obeying Jesus, the man went away sad. The man was very wealthy, and Jesus had exposed the true "god" of this man's life through His invitation to give it all up and follow Him. Even though this man had been doing right things all his life, he had not made God the first love of his heart. That place belonged to his money and possessions. Jesus invited him to pursue the one thing that matters in life: following Jesus. But the man would have to give up what had a hold on his heart. If Jesus isn't the one thing in your heart and life, rest assured that something else is.

King David knew this truth. He chose the right thing, the one thing. In Psalm 27, David declared, "*One thing* I have asked from the LORD, that I shall seek: that I may dwell in the house of the LORD all the days of my life, to behold the beauty of the LORD and to meditate in His temple" (v. 4 NASB). David knew the one thing that really mattered wasn't defeating his enemies or reigning as king. It wasn't having a great reputation for his strength and bravery or being feared by many as a man of war. David knew that pursuing the presence of God and beholding the beauty of God mattered more than anything else.

Remember: What you behold, you become. David wanted to be like his Father God. And even though David made some devastating mistakes in his life, he kept coming back to the one thing. God honored David in some pretty incredible ways, such as making David king, giving him amazing victories over his enemies, and choosing his family line to be the one to birth Jesus. But something God said about David really strikes a chord in my heart more than all the blessings. It's something I desire to one day be said of me. God said that David was a man after His own heart (1 Samuel 13:14). Wow.

From singing songs of praise to God in the shepherd's field to the throne room of the palace, David gave God first place in his heart—in private and in public. The more I ponder this, the more I ask myself: *What has first place in my heart? Have I made pursuing God the* one thing *in my life?*

I encourage you to take a moment and pray through these questions for yourself. God's Holy Spirit will help you find the answers, not in a condemning or angry way but in an invitation, like with the rich man. *Lay all that down . . . follow Me.* He might tell you something like what He said to Martha: *You are worried and distracted by many things, but only one thing is necessary . . . come sit with Me and learn from Me.*

A true Jesus rebel will put first things first and pursue the one thing that truly matters in this life and the next. And trust me when I say that you *really* have to rebel against the pull of this world to do it. You must stand your ground against temptations and distractions and self-focus. You will have to say no to other opportunities and pursuits so you can say *yes* to the one thing, to Jesus. Yeah, you'll be a rebel, and you'll probably be mocked or ridiculed for it. That's okay. So was Jesus. And the servant is not above the Master, right? What an honor to follow in His footsteps and share in His sufferings.

PRIORITIES OF LIFE

I have many days that are filled from morning to night with important tasks, interviews, rehearsals, etc. I bet you can relate to that level of busyness. Some days I feel overwhelmed by the coming day's work and jump right into the long list of what I need to get done. The next task before me becomes the most important thing, one after the other, until I fall into bed exhausted at night.

I don't like days like that. Maybe I did accomplish a lot, perhaps I ticked every item off my list . . . but my list was flawed from the start.

If you are a list person like me, then let's use that to our advantage. In fact, I think this could be helpful to everyone, list lover or not. I have learned that the more overwhelmed I feel, the more desperately I need my time with God. Not that I always succeed, mind you. But I'm learning, just like you. And one thing that can help is a list (or three). It helps me to stop and remember my priorities not just for that day but for life. Then I write down two to three items that are nonnegotiable for me that day. This is the "have-to-do" list. After that, I make a list of important tasks I want to do that day but won't cause the end of the world if they get pushed to tomorrow. This is the "want-to-do" list. Finally, if there's time, I make a list of activities that would be great to accomplish or only matter if I have spare time. This is my "wish-to-do" list. You can probably tell that I start with the have-to-do list and work the others around it. At the top of that list is my time with God. In that time, I submit my lists to Him. They mean nothing if the items on them aren't even in His plan for me that day (or ever!).

I've heard many people say that they don't spend time with God each day because they are too busy. I've used that excuse in the past too. It feels so true as we run around frantically doing many important things. But it isn't true. You and I have the same number of hours in a day that humans have always had. The issue is how we are filling them. Do you get out of bed and put first things first, or do you run straight to to-do lists, work, or scrolling on your phone, like I sometimes fall into? Do you prioritize your days so that you accomplish what matters most to you? It won't just happen on its own. You must be very intentional and determined. You have to say no to other things so you can focus on the *one thing*. Make that nonnegotiable "have-to-do" list, my friend, and let the rest fall around it. That may feel a little scary to you, but I promise it will be okay. In fact, it will be better than okay, and I'd like to tell you how I know that.

RULES FOR LIFE

In 2024, I went on a little beach getaway for my birthday with my mom; my sister, Liz; and our best friends—Aunt Nini (my mom's best friend, Jenna) and her two daughters, Emma and Sarah. It was wonderful and relaxing. I highly recommend a girls' trip to the beach! But it was the day before everyone arrived that shifted my life.

I decided to get there a day early and spend that day alone with God. I could feel stress and weariness building up, and I knew I needed to set aside time and sit at Jesus' feet. If you know me at all or read my first book, you know how being by the ocean helps connect me with God. So I took my Bible and the book I was reading, *Practicing the Way* by John Mark Comer, and sat on the beach for hours. I worshipped, read, listened, and allowed the Holy Spirit to minister to my soul. That day, the Lord showed me that I wasn't putting first things first in all areas of my life, which was leading to my being burned out and run-down. I felt convicted, in the very best way, to make some lasting changes in my life. Essentially, it was time to make some lists for *life*, not just daily lists.

In *Practicing the Way*, Comer focuses on three core principles: being with Jesus, becoming like Him, and doing as He did. He also encourages establishing rules for life, focused on creating a framework to help you truly put first things first. As I read and followed the Lord's promptings in my heart, I realized I needed to create some rules for my life that were biblically based and would help me keep my priorities in line. I know we're called to love God first and to love others, so how could I structure my life to actually do that daily, monthly, and yearly?

Right away, I felt the Lord calling me to set a rule around my Sabbath rest and my time alone with Him. I want God to be my one thing in this life, and that means I need to protect my time alone with Him. This quote from the book really hit home: "Once we are rested, the quiet is where we go to find God. Because it's there, in the quiet, that the inner roar of our world of noise—the distraction, the chaos, and all the lies—fades away, and what shimmers in its place is the peace and presence of God."[1] I can't get to the peace and presence of God unless I set aside time alone with Him, where in rest and quietness I can hear His voice and receive His truth. I'm desperate to be flooded with the peace and presence of God.

So I wrote down a rule for myself to protect Sundays as my Sabbath from that point on, as much as possible, and if I couldn't, to set aside another day of the week. And not long after that, I took an action step, because what is the point of a rule for life without follow-through? I called my team and told them that I would not be touring on Sundays any longer if it was in my power to choose. And if I couldn't avoid a Sunday concert, then I would need another day of the week set apart for God. My weekdays and even my weekends are packed with writing, recording, touring, and so much more. I wanted and needed a day with God each week that was protected from life's distractions.

I also felt led to set some parameters for loving others better. My public music ministry is a wonderful way to do this on a large scale, but God showed me that the personal, one-on-one loving service was lacking. I decided that I would start pouring into others outside my public ministry. I volunteered to work in the nursery at my church on Sundays, I started a Bible study in my home for other young women, and I began mentoring a young lady. Friends, please hear me when I say this: I am not telling you this to get praise or toot my own horn. I simply hope it inspires you to hear my personal story so that you, too, can set biblical rules for your life.

That day on the beach with God was all about learning to rest and obey. As the Lord showed me steps to realign my life, I could choose to obey or not. He taught me more about my need to rest in His presence and not to allow other things, no matter how good they are, to get in the way. Some other choices I made that day were to start doing digital fasts and to begin and end my days with Jesus. Although I'm not always perfect at it, I aim to begin my day worshipping and reading the Word and then spend at least ten minutes before bed with Jesus, thanking Him for all His blessings that day.

How do I know that putting first things first makes your life better? Because it happened to me. Over the last year, as I've put these rules into practice, my life is better—more fulfilled, less stressful, more peaceful, less anxious. And through it all, I have grown closer to God and to other people. I live in the moment better than I used to. I have a well of God's blessing and love in my life from which to love others better.

I am well aware that I have not arrived. In truth, I have a long way to go, as I continue to learn and practice and pursue better. This isn't a one-and-done kind of decision. Each day, I choose how to fill the hours of that day. Will I take those few moments to align my priorities, or will I jump right into busyness and productivity? The longer I practice this, the more I love it and the more I want to do it.

You, too, can make these choices. Whether you're a brand-new follower of Jesus or you've been walking with Him for a long time, there is always *more*. We can always pursue Him better. We will never reach the end of His infinite love. We will be discovering the awesome aspects of God's character far into eternity.

THY WILL BE DONE

An honest pursuit of Jesus will require us to lay aside what hinders us. Just like we talked about at the beginning of the book, we must lay our lives down in order to live for Jesus. He cannot be our one thing if our hearts are set on anything else above Him.

Even Jesus chose this path. He chose to lay aside His divinity and become a man. He daily obeyed Father God, empowered by the Holy Spirit. And when it came down to the culmination of His mission on earth, He laid aside His own will to do the will of God. The night before He went to the cross to take all our sin, Jesus went to a garden to pray. Scripture tells us He was in agony as He prayed (Luke 22:44). Think about that for a moment. Can you even imagine what that must have been like? In the face of certain torture and pain like we will never know, Jesus chose the ultimate obedience of laying down His life. In verse 42, we read His words: "Father, if You are willing, remove this cup from Me; yet not My will, but Yours be done" (NASB).

This is vital, friends. We must lay down our own will, our own desires, our own lives. We choose instead God's will, God's desires, and God's life in us. The choice is hard because our flesh and human nature war against it. But the reward is beyond anything we can imagine—eternal life with God in pure bliss, joy, and peace. Nothing could be better. And life on this earth is better when we choose the way of Jesus—even when it is hard, which will happen often. Praise God that we do not have to rely on our own strength to walk this out. Let's remember how Jesus showed us to pray in Matthew 6:9–13:

> This, then, is how you should pray:
>
> "Our Father in heaven,
> hallowed be your name,
> your kingdom come,
> your will be done,
> on earth as it is in heaven.
> Give us today our daily bread.
> And forgive us our debts,
> as we also have forgiven our debtors.
> And lead us not into temptation,
> but deliver us from the evil one."

We could spend a long time studying this prayer, but let's focus in on one line for now: "your will be done." This is to be our aim and our prayer. God's will is *not* done when we're too busy doing our own will or the will of others. And God's will is perfect, even if we don't understand it in the moment. Doing His will isn't always easy, but it is right and good and just. It is important to realize that we cannot do His will on our own. It is much too great and awesome for us to accomplish without Him. We are meant to live this life of obedience empowered by the Holy Spirit, just like Jesus did. Let's be like Jesus and lay aside our own will for the will and the glory of Almighty God. This is a goal worth pursuing.

A FACE LIKE FLINT

"For the Lord God helps Me, therefore, I am not disgraced; therefore, I have made My face like flint, and I know that I will not be ashamed" (Isaiah 50:7 NASB).

No matter what we face in this life, we can live with confidence in the Lord and in the help He gives us. Because He helps us, we do not need to feel disgraced or ashamed. We can turn our faces like flint and stand firm in the Lord. What does it mean to turn your face like flint? Well, flint is a hard and durable stone. This beautiful metaphor shows us that we are to be determined, durable, and steadfast in the face of opposition.

Not because *we* are strong but because *God* is strong. We become strong and confident because of what He has done. It is only through His help that we can remain true and resolute. Our faces do not need to be downcast in shame or disgrace.

Do you know what else flint does? It can start a fire. If you strike it just right, sparks fly. I know this because my brother, Jacob, had many flint fire starters when he was young and loved to start fires with them. He appreciated the challenge he experienced from starting a fire with just a stone and a spark. It built his confidence in his abilities to survive and protect his loved ones in any setting. One time, he started a roaring fire in our fireplace on Christmas morning. He shut the glass doors to prevent the sparks from flying out, and we all sat down to open gifts together. A few minutes later, the glass doors suddenly shattered into a million pieces! Jacob's fire was so hot that it broke out the doors of the fireplace! And it all started from a little spark that came flying off his flint.

Let's return to the idea of setting our faces like flint. This may be my own interpretation, but I can't help but think that when we obey God and stand firm in Him, we can ignite fires that blaze for His glory. Fires of revival and worship will start when God's people lay themselves aside and love God with all they have and love others with His love. May we live our lives in such a way that we spark fires of revival in the hearts of everyone we meet!

I must warn you, friends, that the more you live for God, the more the Enemy will resist you and the world will hate you. You may be misunderstood, maligned, mistreated, and more. Do not allow the darkness to overshadow the light you carry, the light of Jesus. Do not let the hate of the world snuff out your love. Do not return evil for evil. Set your face like flint and carry the good news of Jesus to this lost and dying world! God wants everyone to be saved, and He's sending you and me to share His love with the world (1 Timothy 2:4). He sends us all. He sends us to other countries, and He sends us to the grocery store. He sends us into classrooms and into boardrooms. Wherever you go, you bring the good news of the gospel of peace.

DO NOT GROW WEARY

Do you sometimes feel disheartened by the growing darkness in this world? Do you grow weary from the fight or simply from the busyness of life? So do I, my friend. There are times when I wonder if it will ever let up! It feels like one battle after another, both personal and in the world. The attacks on truth are growing bolder and more ruthless. There is so much false and twisted information coming at us from all angles that we often don't know what is real and what is fake. And AI only makes it worse, with its fake videos and plethora of information just seconds away. But who is filtering that information? We seem to be at the mercy of the algorithm, which people with agendas have created. And I don't think many of those agendas are based on truth and love. I say all of this to acknowledge that it is easy to grow weary and discouraged. We've all been there.

I cannot say that I have the be-all and end-all answer to this because I am still maturing in my faith right along with you, but I will tell you what I've learned. When I lose hope and feel overwhelmingly discouraged, I know that somewhere inside, I've believed a lie. God is the God of hope. He can solve any problem and has a plan so good that we cannot even imagine it. He is sovereign and all-powerful. And in the end, all will be made right. If I've lost hope, I've lost sight of who He really is.

And when I grow weary, it usually means I've started relying on my own strength and am neglecting my quiet time with God. Just like the quote from *Practicing the*

Way said, it is in that place of rest and quiet that I find the peace and presence of God. When my soul feels like loud static noise that won't quit and constant anxiety brewing underneath, that's my warning sign: time to get alone with God. Don't hesitate. Run to Him.

Therefore, my encouragement to you is that when you feel discouraged, hopeless, worn down, and weary, that is not the time to work harder or hustle more. That is the time to slow down and sit at the feet of Jesus. Remind yourself from the Word who He is. Rest in the quiet joy of His presence and let Him fill you with peace. The world says to work harder, to do more. Resist that. Rebel against it. God says, "Be still, and know that I am God" (Psalm 46:10). When the warning light of your soul comes on, pursue the Lord above all else. He is the only true answer. He is the one thing that will fulfill and sustain you.

It is through reliance on and pursuit of God that we will be able to stay strong, stand firm, and turn our faces as flint, come what may. It is through His power and presence that we do not grow weary to the point of giving up, but we press on in our pursuit, relentless and determined. God promises an amazing reward to those who keep pressing on in this way. Galatians 6:9 says, "Let us not become weary in doing good, for at the proper time we will reap a harvest if we do not give up." God promises that, in His timing, we will reap a harvest from our hard work, just like a farmer who reaps a great crop after months of tilling the soil, planting seeds, pulling weeds, and watering.

Did you know that the old adage "you reap what you sow" comes straight from the Word of God? In fact, it is found right before the verse I just quoted: "Do not be deceived: God cannot be mocked. A man reaps what he sows" (v. 7). Every day, we are sowing seeds, either for our flesh and sinful desires or to please the Spirit of God. Every day, we get to decide. What are you sowing? What harvest will you reap? Have you ever wondered about that? Farmers are very intentional about what seeds they plant, where they plant, and when they plant. It all matters. So do your daily choices. Do not grow weary or give up on planting the seeds that lead to eternal rewards and a harvest of blessing.

If we are going through our days with only the present moment and pleasure on our minds, we will never sow seeds with eternity as our focus. We will always pick the easy route because of our human nature. It takes intentional choice and relentless determination to pursue the greater things of God that lead to eternal rewards.

Rebecca Springer wrote a precious book in the nineteenth century about her vision of heaven. In it she quotes her brother-in-law, who is guiding her through heaven. He says to her, "If only we realized while we are mortals that day by day we are building for eternity. How different our lives in many ways would be! Every gentle word, every generous thought, every unselfish deed will become a pillar of eternal beauty in the life to come."[2] This beautiful thought gives me excitement for our eternal reward, when I will see Jacob again and see Jesus face-to-face. These words also challenge me deeply. I think of how often we live for the temporary pleasures, comforts, and rewards of this life. It is so easy to lose sight of eternity and to focus on getting what I want now. I pray that God will imprint this truth on my heart and mind, and on yours as well. May we live each day with the reality of eternity driving our every decision. May we live a life pleasing to God in all our public and private moments.

BE RELENTLESS

Unfortunately, we live in a world focused on immediate gratification and ultimate comfort. For many people, if they have to wait on something or if it makes them uncomfortable, they're out. They don't want it. We see it in churches today, too, where the pastors are so afraid to make people uncomfortable that they water down the truth. We see it in youth and adults alike who are so used to getting what they want in two days or less that no one knows how to wait any longer. Those are just a couple out of countless examples I could give. In our world, patience is a fleeting virtue; *discomfort* is almost considered a bad word.

But our God does not bow to the impatient timetable of our desires or the craving for comfort we all seem to gravitate toward. Praise God that Jesus did not give in to those temptations or make His own comfort more important than His mission from God. The kingdom of God is not like that. Heaven forbid we try to cram the kingdom of God into our puny little worldview and cultural bias. Heaven forbid indeed. Be ready to wait on the Lord, to get out of your comfort zone, and to lay aside your personal preferences in this amazing journey with God. We cannot be ones who shrink back or give up. That is not what Jesus followers are meant to be. We should be the bravest, boldest, most loving, and most relentless people on the planet!

Let's decide what really matters and go for it with

everything we have. Let's rebel against our culture of comfort and self-indulgence and instead choose to lay ourselves down for others. Let's refuse to give in to hopelessness and discouragement and fear and instead choose to trust God and believe who He says He is!

A true rebel for Jesus will relentlessly pursue the things of God above all else. We will lay it all down for the one thing that truly matters. We will lay down our very lives and our will for the glory of God and His kingdom.

This is my encouragement to you and to myself. Just like the apostle Paul said in Philippians 3:13–14: "Brothers, I do not consider myself to have taken hold of it. But *one thing* I do: Forgetting what is behind and reaching forward to what is ahead, I *pursue* as my goal the prize promised by God's heavenly call in Christ Jesus" (HCSB).

Do you feel it welling up inside, like I do right now? He is calling you to something greater.

TURNING OUR HEARTS TO JESUS

Holy Father,

I feel You stirring inside me, and I want to answer. Holy Spirit, lead me and guide me. I want to say as David did that You are my one thing. I want to passionately and relentlessly pursue You, God, every day of my life. Please show me where the little pebbles of this life are filling places only You should fill. Please speak to me about what You are calling me to, and give me courage to step out in faith. I know You say to me the same words You have said to so many: Lay it all down and follow Me. I will follow You, even if the whole world goes the other way. I choose You, Jesus, as my one thing. I choose a life of passionate and relentless pursuit of You. Thank You that You first pursued me and saved me so I can now live my life for You. I will spend all my days saying thank You. You deserve it all.

Amen.

CHAPTER 10

A REBEL'S HEART TO PLEASE GOD

As a child and a teen, I avoided conflict like the plague. I hated to ruffle anyone's feathers or cause a scene. It tore me up inside to think that someone was upset with me, especially my parents. I was the ultimate rule follower and peacekeeper, trying with all my might to make everyone around me happy.

But the truth of the matter is that we can never, not even for a second, please everyone. It is an impossible and ridiculous goal if you stop to think about it. People have such polarizing beliefs that if you cater to one side, the other side gets offended. If you follow your friends, your parents probably aren't pleased. If you obey your parents, some friends think you're lame. And the list goes on. No matter how frantically we work to keep the peace by making everyone happy, we're on a fool's errand. There is one path to peace, and that is through the Prince of Peace Himself, Jesus Christ.

So the real questions aren't, *How do I make people happy?* or *How do I keep the peace?* Instead, realizing that you can never please everyone, you must ask yourself: *Who am I trying to please?* And knowing that real peace comes only through Jesus, we must ask: *Am I making real peace or protecting a pretend peace?* Real peace comes through Jesus and always involves honesty and humility. It doesn't mean avoiding conflict but rather wading into it carrying the Word and the love of God. The goal is restoration. Pretend peace is an illusion based on self-protection and pride. It compromises with evil to protect people's carefully crafted images or to avoid discomfort and pain.

God chose to reconcile the world to Himself through Jesus and has given us the assignment to bring this good news of peace to everyone. As 2 Corinthians 5:19 says, "God was in Christ reconciling the world to Himself, not counting their trespasses against them, and He has committed to us the word of reconciliation" (NASB1995).

We get to partner with God in the greatest peace-making mission of all time! We are called to lay our lives down for Jesus and follow His example. He never once tells us to protect ourselves or to make sure to keep everyone happy. In fact, He warned us that following Him means we will be persecuted and that even our friends and family may turn against us. So let's also ask ourselves this question: *Am I obeying God and joining with Him in His ministry of reconciliation . . . or am I too worried about upsetting people and too concerned with what they'll think of me?* Let me be clear—any peace that doesn't start and end with Jesus is not real peace. Don't let the world or the media fool you. It's an illusion and a trap.

COMING TO MY SENSES

I never even knew that I was living a life of people-pleasing until I neared the age of twenty. When my first manager quit, it sent me into a temporary tailspin of fear, but out of that fear, I quickly began to wake up to the real situation I'd been in. I believe God used that time to reveal to me how much I had been trying to please others—to the point that I wasn't putting God's direction first in my life. I used to lie in bed at night unable to sleep because I was worried sick over displeasing my manager and my label. I was extremely afraid to make a mistake or upset them, which would give them a bad opinion of me. Or so I assumed.

Then in 2021, I started seeing my counselor, and it took about five minutes of her explaining people-pleasing to me before I realized how ingrained this sin was in my life and my personality. For the first time, I realized how unhealthy it is to try to make everyone around you happy. I saw how I wasn't being honest with the people in my life when I told them only what I thought they wanted to hear or went along with their desires and ignored what God had put in my own heart. I had to learn how to speak the truth in love, starting with my family and friends and expanding from there. Once I knew how dangerous people-pleasing can be, I didn't want any part of it. I realized that when we are focused on pleasing others more than on pleasing God, we are putting those people and their opinions in place of God. That's idolatry!

That began my journey out of people-pleasing and peacekeeping and into pleasing God first and becoming a peacemaker. I still have a lot to learn, but those initial first shifts set me free from the opinions of others in a major way and changed my life for the better.

PEACEKEEPER VERSUS PEACEMAKER

The definitions of the words *peacekeeper* and *peacemaker* are basically contained within the words themselves. But let's discuss them for a moment to be sure we're all on the same page. If you're a peacekeeper, you are working hard to *keep* peace. For our purposes, this means trying to keep all sides happy so that conflicts don't spring up. As we've already discussed, that is an impossible goal. You sacrifice truth and purpose for the sake of false peace and conflict avoidance. I was queen of conflict avoidance, let me tell you. And it did *not* bring peace. I may have avoided some temporary conflicts or uncomfortable conversations, but my soul was not at peace. It also set me up for greater problems in the future. Ignoring an issue does not make it go away. It just gives it time to grow and fester. Eventually you'll have to face it. I can't tell you the number of times I've finally shared my true feelings or an opinion on something with my mom and her reaction is, "Why didn't you tell me sooner?" And I wish I had because it would have saved us so much pain.

A peacemaker, on the other hand, is someone willing to wade into conflict and *make* peace. This is someone who speaks truth in love, listens to others with humility, and works to bring the kingdom of God everywhere he or she goes. Initially this can be less comfortable, but it brings lasting resolution and restoration when it is successful. Not everyone is willing to go to this place of peacemaking, so no matter your best efforts, you won't always be able to make peace with someone else. Even Jesus won't force another person into making peace with God. We all have a choice.

When I think about being a peacemaker, I always think of my sweet mama. God has put a boldness and strength inside her petite body that amazes me and surprises most people she meets. She has been a huge example to me because she isn't afraid to face conflicts or misunderstandings head-on. If an issue arises with others, she is usually the first to say, "Let's go straight to them and figure this out!" When I was younger, I felt resistant and anxious about her desire to face a problem in that way, but now I am extremely grateful for it.

My parents have both lived out the example of how to be a peacemaker by practicing it with me and my siblings. When they needed to confront us with a problem we were having or to find out why we were upset with or rebelling against them, they sat us down to talk. Mom would pull out her notebook and pen, which meant it was time for business. They asked us questions about how we were feeling and why we were behaving badly. She faithfully wrote down our key points and shared them back with us to make sure she was hearing us. Sometimes, Mom and Dad would see the situation in a new light after hearing our side. But most often, they helped us to see the truth through these conversations. They came to us with love, wisdom, and truth. We talked about the hard things in a way that made us kids feel understood and valued.

But they did not stop there. They faithfully redirected us where our young minds were not seeing the situation correctly or were clouded by the Enemy's lies. They worked through the conflict toward a solution. And it *was* work. Peace isn't made accidentally or passively. It must be pursued and fought for. As Paul said in Romans 14:19, "So then we pursue the things which make for peace and the building up of one another" (NASB1995).

Are there situations in your own life that you need to face head-on and places where you should pursue peace? Maybe it's time to grab your notebook and pen and sit down for a heart-to-heart with someone. I know it may feel very scary for some of you. Know that the Holy Spirit will be with you and will lead you if you ask and allow Him. For others of you, the confrontation might not be your struggle, but rather the ability to do it with humility and love. Once again, it's God's Spirit who will give you the self-control and the love to have these hard conversations in a way that honors God and others.

As I reflect on my parents' example, I see some key points to peacemaking that I want to apply better in my own life. Perhaps these will also inspire you. First, they did not compromise with sin or with lies from the Enemy. If they saw any of that in us (or even in themselves), they called it out and dealt with it. Second, they were willing to face conflict to reach real peace. Sometimes conflict is necessary to reach resolution if we walk through it in a healthy way. I have found that when I practice this, the relationship usually ends up stronger than it started. Third, my parents came in a spirit of love and humility with a real desire for restoration. Finally, they resisted the attempts of the Enemy to destroy our family and their kids. They were tenacious in their fight for our souls and for our family. They did not stay silent or passive or take the easy way out. We've had many painful conversations, but the goal has always been restoration. They keep working toward that goal no matter how difficult or how long it takes.

RESIST EVIL

We are told by God to resist the devil. I believe that means resisting all his evil schemes and lies. We are not called to keep the peace and quietly sit by while the devil steals, kills, and destroys people all around us. We should never compromise with or ignore evil to protect our own image or our own comfort. That is putting our image, reputation, and self-comfort before God. Once again, that's idolatry.

And to be clear, I'm not talking about choosing physical violence or hateful resistance. When I say we resist evil, that means we do not give in to it. We don't make deals with it. We don't let it happen without speaking up against it. We don't sit idly by while evil has a heyday. Jesus didn't. With this in mind, let's remember some of the things Jesus did.

When greedy men filled His Father's house to make money by cheating God's people, Jesus sat down, and with intentional purpose, He fashioned a whip. Then He used that whip to drive them out of the temple. He did not allow evil to make its home in His Father's house.

When Satan tempted Jesus to bow down and worship him in return for all the kingdoms of the earth, Jesus did not make a deal with him.

When the Pharisees opposed His teachings, Jesus did not pretend to have peace with them. He made it clear what side they were on when He called them whitewashed tombs and sons of the devil.

When Satan worked through Peter's words to tempt Jesus into self-protection and avoiding the cross, Jesus would not listen. He stopped the conversation in its tracks and made it clear that this line of thinking was from Satan! Jesus did not mess around with evil. He did not turn a blind eye. He called it what it was, and He spoke truth.

If you really want to know what a peacemaker looks like, you must study the life of Jesus. He was the ultimate peacemaker, the Prince of Peace. He came to restore humanity's broken relationship with God by entering the conflict as a human. He spoke hard truths that polarized many people. He encountered anger, hostility, false accusations, and violence to the point of death, but He did not return evil for evil. He did not participate in it. And nothing stopped Him from achieving His goal of reconciling man to God. Nothing. We know that God desires a relationship with everyone and was willing to lay down His life for it, just as the Word says: "For it was the Father's good pleasure for all the fullness to dwell in Him, and through Him to reconcile all things to Himself, having *made peace* through the blood of His cross" (Colossians 1:19–20 NASB1995).

Evil hates truth, and Jesus is the living, breathing truth. Jesus was hated and still is. Remember that the devil is the father of lies? So of course he rages against truth. And we know from John 8:32 that "you will know the truth, and the truth will make you free" (NASB1995). The Enemy wants us enslaved to fear through people-pleasing and compromise. But Jesus' truth sets us free and gives us peace. There is no real peace without truth.

Escaping the snare of people-pleasing and instead becoming a peacemaker will take courage, my friends. Sometimes speaking up for what is right is scary. You may be afraid of rejection or of being made fun of. It might terrify you to think of losing friends or your reputation. Maybe you fear you'll get fired. In this current world, all those things are possible. But your Father in heaven will lead you and guide you and provide for you. You can trust Him with the results. You can trust Him with your reputation. You can trust Him with your very life. Turn your heart back to Jesus and remember how much He loves you. Let His love for you motivate you to carry out His great mission.

THE FEAR OF MAN VERSUS THE FEAR OF GOD

People-pleasing and *the fear of man* are closely connected concepts. If you're trying to please people, it is linked to being afraid of what they will say about you, do to you, or think of you. Out of that fear, you try to keep them happy with you. But those actions are all centered around *you*, and that's the problem.

The Bible makes it clear over and over again that rather than fearing man, we are supposed to have a deep and reverential fear of God. As John Bevere puts it, "To fear God is to *reverence* and be in complete *awe* of Him."[1] Having the right view of who God is and humbling ourselves in reverence and awe of Him is where we start. Proverbs 9:10 says, "The fear of the LORD is the beginning of wisdom, and the knowledge of the Holy One is understanding" (NASB).

It really matters who you're trying to please. I suggest that you revisit the question I posed earlier in this chapter: *Who am I trying to please?* Yourself? Other people? God? In his book *The Awe of God*, John Bevere goes into great depth about what the fear of the Lord is and why it matters so very much for a Christ follower. Here is one of his important points that relates to what I'm saying: "We should keep this truth before us at all times: *You will serve whom you fear!* If you fear God, you'll obey God. If you fear man, you'll ultimately obey man's desires."[2]

I don't know about you, but I tremble at the thought of putting man's desires before God's in my life. Yet it can be so hard! What if honoring God means I make others mad or I offend them? What if they hate me or ridicule me? What if they attack me online or reject me? Do you have the same thoughts and fears? Okay. *What if?* Follow that train of thought. Face it head-on and be ready to decide. And compare it to this: *What if I don't obey God and instead make people's opinions more important to me than God's?* If you've read the Bible much, you know that putting other people or things in God's place in our lives does not end well for us.

The apostle Paul made this issue very clear in Galatians 1:10 when he said, "Am I now seeking the favor of men, or of God? Or am I striving to please men? If I were still trying to please men, I would not be a bond-servant of Christ" (NASB1995). How can we fully serve Christ if we are seeking the favor of men? We can't.

I want to have a healthy and reverential fear of God in my heart, which motivates me to honor and obey Him *no matter what*. I want to be willing to lay down my pride, reputation, comfort, and self-protection to fulfill the destiny God has for my life. It can be hard and scary, but friends, think of the eternal reward! What do you want to do in response to these challenges? It's time for an intentional decision: Please man or please God? Fear man or fear God?

What God offers you in return is so much greater than anything you could ever give up for Him. What He has already done for you is so much greater than anything the world has to offer. He is worthy of it all—your life, your reputation, your comfort, your everything!

LIVING, DYING, AND SPEAKING UP FOR CHRIST

When I think of a modern example of someone willing to live (and die) for Christ, a true peacemaker for the kingdom of God, I think of Charlie Kirk. He has had a tremendous impact on the young people of my generation and on me. He demonstrated what it means to face conflict head-on with humility and love by having personal conversations about tough topics with young adults across the country. He often said that it's when we quit having face-to-face conversations that bad things happen and violence results.[3]

Friends, I am writing these words just three days after the assassination of Charlie Kirk, and my soul is on fire. The world just watched a peacemaking man who loved Jesus with everything in him be assassinated for speaking the truth. I've listened to countless conversations Charlie had over the years, and I have never once seen him be hateful or cruel. He did not incite violence; he invited people into conversation. His heart burned for the youth of America to hear and recognize truth. He preached the gospel of Jesus Christ everywhere he went, his faith informing everything he did. He did not spew racist or bigoted ideology. Those who claim he did are manipulating opinions of others by taking comments out of context and splicing sound bites. If you don't believe me, do some research of your own and listen to full conversations. Don't believe the lies that have circulated about this godly man. Watch and listen for yourself, and ask God to reveal truth to you.

From all I have seen and heard, I firmly believe that Charlie Kirk was murdered because he spoke the truth. His life, and now his death, point to Jesus Christ as Lord and Savior. He wasn't scared or intimidated to say so. He was dangerous to the Enemy, and he was killed for his faith. He died a martyr's death. Right in front of the whole world.

Within days of Charlie's death, so much changed. People were coming out in droves to say that they turned back to God because of Charlie's message. People woke up to the battle of good versus evil that is all around us. And the way Christians reacted to this tragedy revealed quite a bit about what they valued most. I pray that by the time you read these words, this movement back to God will have only grown and multiplied.

Personally, I chose to publicly honor the life and death of Charlie Kirk and to encourage others to do the same by boldly living for Jesus in a world that feels so dark right now. In response, some people spewed words of hate or judgment toward me. Some people unfollowed me immediately. Guess what? I do not care one bit. I'm not saying I don't care about those people. I actually do, and I pray that their hearts encounter God's love in a life-changing way. I am saying that I do not care if the world, or even professing Christians, turn against me for speaking up for Jesus. I signed up for that. I'm not in this for my own reputation. I do this for Jesus and for Him alone. What people think of me is none of my business.

Sadly, I'm watching pastors, worship leaders, artists, and public figures either stay silent in the face of this evil or try to walk a tightrope of people-pleasing. Rather than simply denouncing the evil that took the life of a man who proclaimed the name of Jesus, they add caveats about not fully agreeing with him *before* they say anything else. Are you kidding me? They massage their words in a vain attempt to make everyone happy and not offend the masses. That tells me that they are more concerned about not losing followers and protecting their image than they are about resisting the devil and standing up for what is right. I've been in that place of trying to please people. But I've also repented and turned from that sin, as I talked about earlier. I cannot and will not judge their hearts, but I do see their actions, and I will call it what it is. If you cannot put your reputation aside and denounce the public execution of a man who respectfully dialogued and spoke about Jesus—without adding words to protect yourself and please other people—then I'd say you are compromising with evil for the sake of your own pride. I'd say you fear man more than you fear God.

Now, I know most of you reading this book are not public figures with a platform to protect. But you can ask yourself what your greatest motivation was in how *you* reacted to the assassination of Charlie Kirk or any of the many other evil events of our day. And you can examine the reactions of those you follow and listen to on a regular basis. Perhaps you need to reconsider who has influence in your life. I beg of you to be sure you are listening to voices who speak truth with boldness, who are not ashamed of the gospel of Jesus Christ, and who resist evil without compromise. If someone puts protecting their reputation as their first response or stays silent about evil, reconsider letting them have influence in your heart and mind. We must all use great wisdom and discernment about what and who we allow to hold sway in our hearts. The world grows darker and deception is more rampant than ever before. Stay vigilant, friends.

WE DON'T SHRINK BACK

Now more than ever before in my lifetime, I see the battle between good and evil playing out all around me. Do you see it too? Are your eyes open to it? Now is not the time for Christ followers to shrink back. Let us say with the author of Hebrews, "We are not of those who shrink back to destruction, but of those who have faith to the preserving of the soul" (Hebrews 10:39 NASB1995).

This is the time for us to put on the armor of God, to humble ourselves at the feet of Jesus, to stand for truth, and to resist the devil. We must know who God really is and who He calls us to be. Find your worth and identity in Him alone, not in what the world says about you. We must be ready, friends, because the spiritual battle is here and it is now. It is all around us.

Will you let the courage and boldness of God give you strength to wade into the mess and bring the good news of peace in Jesus Christ? You bring the kingdom of God with you. You bring the light of Christ to a dark and dying world. Jesus said, "You are the light of the world. . . . Let your light shine before men in such a way that they may see your good works, and glorify your Father who is in heaven" (Matthew 5:14, 16 NASB1995). Let your light shine in the darkness!

Yes, we will look like rebels and maybe even fanatics. Yes, we will be persecuted and maligned and hated. The Enemy is furious, but God is not scared or worried or even slightly flustered. He is so infinitely greater than everything else, including the Enemy, that no comparison is even possible. All our hope and all our peace are in Jesus, the creator and sustainer of all things. He Himself told us, "These things I have spoken to you so that *in Me* you may have peace. In the world you have tribulation, but take courage; I have overcome the world" (John 16:33 NASB).

I'm not perfect in any of this, but I'm moving forward, following in the dust of my Savior. Will you come with me? Each and every morning, we get to wake up and choose. You are the only one who can decide for you. What do you say? Want to be a rebel for Jesus? Let's do it. When the world goes one way, we will go another. Let's stand our ground and not back down.

And if it comes to it, I pray that we will be ready to lay it all down for Jesus the way Charlie Kirk did, the way all the martyrs through the ages have done. May we all fall so in love with Jesus and be so infused with courage to speak life-giving truth to a dying world that we are not afraid to give up everything for Him. Death is just a doorway to greater life. May we say with the apostle Paul, "to me, to live is Christ, and to die is gain" (Philippians 1:21 NASB).

You, my sweet friend, were born for such a time as this. Your existence at this exact point in history is no coincidence. You were made for this! As we arise in the strength of Christ and take our stand, I have hope for the body of Christ and for the world. May this be our finest hour yet. May revival sweep our nation and the world as we lift high the name of Jesus Christ. For we know that when Christ is lifted up, He will draw all men unto Himself (John 12:32). No matter what happens in this world, let us stand firm with feet planted on the Rock of Ages and lift high the mighty name of Jesus Christ.

Are you with me?

TURNING OUR HEARTS TO JESUS

My dear Lord Jesus,

I am in awe of You. Humbly at Your feet I bow. Fill me with Your Spirit and with Your Love. Fill my mouth with words of truth and my heart with boldness for You. I want to passionately pursue You all my days. I want to sit at Your feet and listen to Your Word. For Your words are life. Jesus, I surrender all—my pride, my reputation, my fears, my past, my future, my life—I lay it all down before the One who is worthy of it all. O Lord, give me ears to hear Your voice, a heart to receive Your love, and strength to obey Your Word. Just like the familiar song says, "I have decided to follow Jesus; no turning back, no turning back."

I love You, O Lord, my strength and my salvation.

In Your mighty name, Jesus, amen.

ACKNOWLEDGMENTS

To my brother, Jacob, in heaven, your life and your love continue to give me strength, especially when the days are hard. You keep me focused on the eternal. I carry you in my heart every day until I see you again. I miss you dearly.

To my parents, thank you for setting an example for me of how to be a follower of Jesus. You both walk out your faith in the most beautiful way, and it is such an inspiration to me.

To my sister and best friend, the one who has stood by me, believed in me, and supported me from the very beginning.

To Marcie, thank you for helping me write this book and for breathing life into every page. Your wisdom, patience, and steady guidance have been such a blessing. I am so grateful to God for you and for the privilege of working alongside you.

Matthew, thank you for every word of encouragement, every moment of support, and every steady presence you have given me in this chapter. You have helped me grow, steadied me when I needed it, and brought out the best parts of who I am. You truly inspire me, and I am so grateful for you.

To Maggie, Ashley, Sara, Grace, and the entire Story House Collective team, thank you for the endless hours of work and support. I couldn't do any of this without you!

To Kyle Olund and the entire team at W Publishing. Thank you for believing in this book and this message. I am so thankful for your support.

My sweet Jesus, thank You for entrusting me with the privilege of proclaiming Your name. I am unworthy, and it's only by Your mercy, Your strength, and Your calling that I am able to do this. May every word honor You and point others to Your love and truth. All glory goes to You alone.

NOTES

CHAPTER 1

1. For more information, see Megan Sauter, "When Was Jesus Born—B.C. or A.D.?" *Biblical Archaeology Society*, June 12, 2024, https://www.biblicalarchaeology.org/daily/people-cultures-in-the-bible/jesus-historical-jesus/when-was-jesus-born-bc-or-ad/.
2. John Eldredge, *Beautiful Outlaw* (FaithWords, 2011), 86.

CHAPTER 4

1. For more information, see John Eldredge, "The Theme for the Year," Wild at Heart, December 31, 2009, https://wildatheart.org/blogs/john/the-theme-of-the-new-year/.

CHAPTER 6

1. Brooke Ligertwood, "We Were Made to Give Glory," June 19, 2020, YouTube, https://www.youtube.com/shorts/LL0BkSQddIk.
2. Andrew Murray, *Humility: The Journey Toward Holiness* (Bethany House Publishers, 2001), 63.

CHAPTER 7

1. John Eldredge, *Walking with God* (Nelson Books, 2008, 2016).

CHAPTER 8

1. John Mark Comer, *The Ruthless Elimination of Hurry* (WaterBrook, 2019), 62.
2. Comer, *The Ruthless Elimination of Hurry*, 135.

CHAPTER 9

1. John Mark Comer, *Practicing the Way* (WaterBrook, 2024), 183.
2. Rebecca Springer, *Within Heaven's Gates* (originally published as *Intra Muros*) (Whitaker House, 1984), 22.

CHAPTER 10

1. John Bevere, *The Awe of God* (W Publishing: 2023), 17.
2. Bevere, *The Awe of God*, 92.
3. NZ Media Watch, "Charlie Kirk: 'When people stop talking . . .'" YouTube, September 11, 2025, 21 sec.

ABOUT THE AUTHOR

ANNE WILSON makes music where faith and country meet—a rare space that lets honesty, grief, and hope live side by side. The Kentucky native first captured hearts as a teen with "My Jesus," a song born from the loss of her older brother, Jacob. The breakout hit became a PLATINUM-certified No. 1 and set Wilson on a path to becoming one of the most distinctive new voices in modern music.

Unapologetically real and grounded in small-town values, Wilson blends bluegrass roots, powerhouse vocals, and faith-driven conviction in a way that feels both rebellious and deeply familiar. Her latest album, *REBEL,* pushes that boundary even further—a bold musical statement shaped by struggle, joy, and the courage to live out her beliefs. Featuring songs like "Rain In The Rearview," "Strong," and "The Cross," the album explores what it means to stand firm in identity even when you don't fit the mold.

Since her Grammy-nominated debut album, *My Jesus,* Wilson has surpassed two billion global streams, made her Grand Ole Opry debut, and completed multiple sold-out headline tours. Whether singing about family, resilience, loss, or unwavering faith, she brings purpose and conviction to every lyric—inviting listeners not just to hear her story but to find their own courage within it.